CARDINAL
REFLECTIONS

Robert Webber

FROM THE LIBRARY OF
THE INSTITUTE FOR
WORSHIP STUDIES
FLORIDA CAMPUS

List of Contributors

Cardinal George Pell, Archbishop of Sydney (Australia), was born on 8 June 1941 in Ballarat, Australia. He was ordained a priest on 16 December 1966 and holds a licentiate in theology from the Urbaniana University of Rome, a master's degree in education from Monash University and a doctorate of philosophy in Church History from the University of Oxford. Cardinal Pell served as Director of the Aquinas Campus of the Institute of Catholic Education (1974–1984) and Principal of the Institute of Catholic Education (1981–1984). He was Episcopal Vicar for Education in the Diocese of Ballarat and a founding member of the Catholic Education Commission of Victoria.

On 21 May 1987 he was ordained an Auxiliary Bishop of the Archdiocese of Melbourne and titular Bishop of Scala.

From 1988–1997 he was Chairman of Caritas Australia. During that same period, he was member of the National Catholic Commission and from 1994-97 he was Secretary to the Bishops' Committee for Education. In 1989, Cardinal Pell was appointed Chairman of the committee charged with setting up the new Australian Catholic University, and in 1991–1995 he served as pro-chancellor of the University's Foundation. From 1985–1987 he was Rector of Corpus Christi College, the Provincial Seminary for Victoria and Tasmania. In 1990, he attended the Synod of Bishops in Rome on the preparation of priests, where he served as one of the Synod spokesmen and on the committee which prepared the final Synod message. He was appointed Apostolic Visitor to the National Seminaries of New Zealand (1994), Papua New Guinea and the Solomon Islands (1995), the Pacific (1996) and Irian Jaya and Sulawesi (1998) by the Congregation for the Evangelization of Peoples in the Vatican.

In November 1998, Cardinal Pell attended the Synod for Oceania. He was appointed by Pope John Paul II to represent the Bishops of Australia and Oceania at the Special Synod for European Bishops in 1999 and the Synod of Bishops held in 2001. In April 2002, he was named President of the *Vox Clara* committee for the English translations of liturgical texts.

Contents

List of Contributors   iv

Introduction   1
George Cardinal Pell
Archbishop of Sydney

Active Participation in the Sacred Liturgy   15
Francis Cardinal Arinze
Prefect of the Congregation of Divine Worship and the Discipline of the Sacraments

Participating in the Sacred Liturgy   27
Jorge A. Cardinal Medina Estévez
Prefect Emeritus of the Congregation of Divine Worship and the Discipline of the Sacraments
Archbishop emeritus of Valparaiso, Chile

Commemorating *Sacrosanctum Concilium* Anniversary Address: The Foundations of Liturgical Reform   45
Francis Eugene Cardinal George, OMI
Archbishop of Chicago

Appendix
Constitution on the Sacred Liturgy *Sacrosanctum Concilium*   59

"Active Participation in the Sacred Liturgy," by Francis Cardinal Arinze, is the keynote address from the 2004 Conference of the Society for Catholic Liturgy. Presented September 23, 2004, in Mundelein, Illinois. Reprinted with permission of The Society of Catholic Liturgy.

"Participating in the Sacred Liturgy," by Jorge A. Cardinal Medina Estévez, is reprinted from *L'Osservatore Romano*, Weekly Edition in English, 1 September 2004, pp. 8–11. Reprinted with kind permission of the publisher.

"*Sacrosanctum Concilium* Anniversary Address: The Foundations of Liturgical Reform," by Francis Eugene Cardinal George, is an address presented at the *Second Vatican Council's Constitution on the Liturgy*, a day-long conference sponsored by the Congregation for Divine Worship and Discipline of the Sacraments (CDW). It was held at the Vatican on December 4, 2003. Reprinted with permission.

The English translation of the Constitution on the Sacred Liturgy *Sacrosanctum Concilium* from *Documents on the Liturgy 1963–1979: Conciliar, Papal, and Curial Texts* © 1982, International Committee on English in the Liturgy, Inc. All Rights Reserved.

CARDINAL REFLECTIONS: ACTIVE PARTICIPATION AND THE LITURGY
© 2005 Archdiocese of Chicago: Liturgy Training Publications, 1800 North Hermitage Avenue, Chicago IL 60622-1101; 1-800-933-1800, fax 1-800-933-7094, e-mail orders@ltp.org. All rights reserved. See our website at www.ltp.org.

HillenbrandBooks is an imprint of Liturgy Training Publications (LTP) and the Liturgical Institute at the University of St. Mary of the Lake (USML). The imprint is focused on contemporary and classical theological thought concerning the liturgy of the Catholic Church. Available at bookstores everywhere, through LTP by calling 1-800-933-1800, or visiting www.ltp.org. Further information about **HillenbrandBooks** is available from the University of St. Mary of the Lake / Mundelein Seminary, 1000 E. Maple Avenue, Mundelein, IL 60060, 847837-4542, or on the web at www.usml.edu/liturgicalinstitute, or e-mail litinst@usml.edu.

Cover photo © AP/Wide World Photos.

Printed in the United States of America.

Library of Congress Control Number: 2005928919

ISBN 1-59525-013-1

CARDINAL REFLECTIONS
Active Participation and the Liturgy

Francis Cardinal Arinze
Francis Cardinal George
Jorge Cardinal Medina Estévez
George Cardinal Pell

HillenbrandBooks

Chicago / Mundelein, Illinois

In 2001 the Holy Father appointed Cardinal Pell the eighth Metropolitan Archbishop of Sydney. He was installed as Archbishop at St. Mary's Cathedral on 10 May 2001.

Curial Membership:
- Family, Justice, and Peace (councils)
- Ordinary Council of the General Secretariat of the Synod of Bishops

Cardinal Francis Arinze, Prefect of the Congregation of Divine Worship and the Discipline of the Sacraments, was born on 1 November 1932 in Eziowelle, a city of the Archdiocese of Onitsha, Nigeria. At the age of 15, he began his secondary studies at the All Hallowa Seminary (Ognissanti) of Nuewi, studies that he concluded in 1950 at Enugu. For the following two years he taught at the same seminary until 1953, when he took up philosophy studies at Bigard Memorial Seminary at Enugu. In 1955 he began to take courses in theology at the Pontifical Urban University. Only three years later he was ordained to the priesthood during a ceremony that took place at the church of the Pontifical Urban University in Rome on 23 November 1958.

From 1961–1962, he was professor of liturgy and also taught logic and basic philosophy at Bigard Memorial Seminary at Enugu. He was then appointed regional secretary for Catholic education for the eastern part of his country. When transferred to London, he took courses at the Institute of Pedagogy, earning a diploma in 1964.

On 6 July 1965 he was appointed to the titular church of Fissiana and named coadjutor to the Archbishop of Onitsha. On 29 August 1965 he was consecrated bishop. Only two years after he was asked to take over the pastoral government of the archdiocese, and on 26 June 1967 he was named archbishop.

In 1979 his brother bishops elected him president of the Catholic Bishops' Conference of Nigeria, which post he filled until 1984, when John Paul II asked him to head as pro-president the Secretariat for Non-Christians (now the Pontifical Council for Interreligious Dialogue).

He remained Archbishop of Onitsha until April 1985, while awaiting the nomination of his successor to assume the pastoral

administration of the Archdiocese. In addition, in 1982 he was elected vice-president for Africa of the United Bible Society.

President of the Pontifical Council for Interreligious Dialogue, 27 May 1985–1 October 2002.

On 8 May 1994, he presided in the capacity of first President Delegate at the solemn closing of the Special Assembly for Africa of the Synod of Bishops at the altar of the Chair of St. Peter's Basilica.

On 24 October 1999 he received a gold medallion from the International Council of Christians and Jews for his "outstanding achievements in inter-faith relations."

He was also a member of the Committee of the Great Jubilee of the Year 2000.

On 1 October 2002 he was nominated Prefect of the Congregation of Divine Worship and the Discipline of the Sacraments.

Curial Membership:
- Doctrine of the Faith, Oriental Churches, Causes of Saints, Evangelization of Peoples (congregations)
- Laity, Christian Unity, Culture (councils)
- International Eucharistic Congresses (committee)
- Ordinary Council of the General Secretariat of the Synod of Bishops
- Special Council for Africa and Special Council for Lebanon of the General Secretariat of the Synod of Bishops

Cardinal Jorge Arturo Medina Estévez, Prefect emeritus of the Congregation of Divine Worship and the Discipline of the Sacraments, was born on 23 December 1926 in Santiago de Chile, Chile. In the same city he did his primary and secondary studies at the *Liceo Alemán* and prior to entering the seminary he attended the law faculty at the Pontifical Catholic University of Chile. He also obtained a baccalaureate in arts and in biology. He entered the major seminary of Santiago and was ordained a priest on 12 June 1954.

In 1955 he received his doctorate in theology. Until 1965 he taught philosophy at the seminary and until 1994 theology at the faculty of the Pontifical Catholic University of Chile, where he also

served for several years as dean. From 1974 to 1985, he was Pro-Grand Chancellor of the same university.

For many years he was canon penitentiary of the metropolitan cathedral of Santiago, and also judge of the ecclesiastical tribunal of Santiago.

He served as a *peritus* at Vatican Council II. He was later a member of the International Theological Commission and the drafting commission for the *Catechism of the Catholic Church*.

On 18 December 1984 he was elected titular Bishop of Tibili and at the same time nominated Auxiliary of Rancagua. He was ordained by John Paul II at St. Peter's Basilica on the Epiphany of 1985.

In 1986 he was nominated Apostolic Administrator of the diocese of Rancagua and on 25 November 1987 he became Bishop. Then on 16 April 1993, he was appointed Bishop of Valparaíso.

In 1992 the Pope nominated him Secretary General of the IV General Conference of Latin American Bishops, celebrated 12–28 October in Santo Domingo. In 1993 he preached the Holy Father's Lenten retreat.

He is the author of many works: books, theological-pastoral booklets and articles on ecclesiological themes, spirituality, and canon law.

His renowned participation in Vatican Council II had earned him in 1996 a *honoris causa* doctorate from the Notre Dame University in Indiana and, due to his teachings and publications, he received a *Doctor Scientiae et honoris causa* from the Pontifical Catholic University of Chile. He was also nominated Chaplain *ad honorem* of the Sovereign Military Order of the Hospital of Saint John of Jerusalem, of Rhodes, and of Malta.

On 21 June 1996 John Paul II appointed him Pro-prefect of the Congregation for Divine Worship and Discipline of the Sacraments. That same day he resigned as bishop of the diocese of Valparaíso and on 19 September 1996 was nominated Archbishop. Created and proclaimed Cardinal by John Paul II in the consistory of 21 February 1998. Deacon, San Saba.

Prefect of the Congregation of Divine Worship and Discipline of the Sacraments, 23 February 1998.

Curial Membership:
- Clergy, Doctrine of the Faith, Bishops (congregations)
- Family, Legislative Texts (councils)
- Latin America, *Ecclesia Dei* (commissions)

Cardinal Francis Eugene George, OMI, Archbishop of Chicago, was born in Chicago, the son of Francis J. George and Julia R. McCarthy, on 16 January 1937. He is the first native of Chicago to become Archbishop of the city.

After attending Saint Paschal Grade School in the north-west of Chicago and the Saint Henry Minor Seminary, Illinois, he entered the Congregation of the Missionary Oblates of Mary Immaculate on 14 August 1957.

He studied theology at the University of Ottawa in Canada and was ordained priest by Bishop Raymond P. Hilliger on 21 December 1963.

Cardinal George pursued undergraduate studies in philosophy at the Catholic University of America in Washington, D.C., and then doctoral studies in philosophy at Tulane University in New Orleans, Louisiana. In these years, he also taught philosophy at the Seminary of the Oblates in Pass Christian, Mississippi (1964–1969), at Tulane University, (1968), and at Creighton University, Omaha, Nebraska (1969–1973).

From 1973 to 1974 he was Provincial Superior of the Midwestern Province of the Oblates at Saint Paul, Minnesota. He was then elected Vicar General of the Oblates and worked in Rome from 1974 to 1986.

He returned to the United States and became coordinator of the Circle of Fellows of the Cambridge Center for the Study of Faith and Culture in Cambridge, Massachusetts (1987–1990).

At that time he pursued doctoral studies in theology at the Pontifical Urban University in Rome, with a specialization in ecclesiology (1988).

Pope John Paul II named him Bishop of Yakima in Washington State on 10 July 1990. He was ordained to the episcopate on 21 September 1990 and was installed as the fifth Bishop of Yakima on the same day.

After five and a half years at Yakima, he was named by Pope John Paul II as Archbishop of Portland, Oregon, on 30 April 1996. He took possession of the See as the ninth Archbishop of Portland on 27 May 1996.

Less than a year later, on 8 April 1997, Pope John Paul II named him the eighth Archbishop of Chicago, since the See had fallen vacant with the death of Cardinal Joseph Bernardin on 14 November 1996.

The installation took place on 7 May 1997, and Archbishop Agostino Cacciavillan, Apostolic Nuncio in the United States of America, presided at the celebration, which took place in Holy Name Cathedral.

He was appointed by the Pope to the Synod of Bishops on Consecrated Life in 1994, and as Delegate and Special Secretary to the American Synod in 1997. He has also served on several Commissions of the National Conference of Catholic Bishops in the United States, including The Church in Latin America (from 1994), Doctrine (1991–1994 and from 1996), Missions (from 1991), the Adhoc Committee to Oversee the Use of the Catechism (from 1995) and the Adhoc Committee on Shrines (from 1992).

From 1994 to 1997 he worked on the Committees on Religious Life and Ministry and the American Board of Catholic Missions within the National Conference of Catholic Bishops.

He has been a consultor for the NCCB on the following commissions: Science and Human Values (1994–1997), Hispanic Affairs (1994–1997), Evangelization (1991–1993). He was also President of the NCCB's Commission for Bishops and Scholars (1992–1994).

He is the representative of the NCCB on the International Commission for English in the Liturgy. He is also on the Council of the Catholic Church Extension Society and of St. Mary of the Lake University, Mundelein, Illinois. He is a member of the Council of Administration of the Catholic University of America (since 1995) and of the Basilica of The National Shrine of the Immaculate Conception (since 1997). He is also a member of the Pontifical Foundation (since 1997) and of the Council of Administration of the Pope John XXIII Center, Boston, Massachusetts (since 1994).

Since 1990 he has been the Episcopal Moderator and member of the Council of the National Catholic Office for Persons with

Disabilities. He brings personal experience to this work, since at the age of 13 he was stricken for five months with poliomyelitis, which caused irreparable damage to his legs.

He was also the Episcopal Moderator of the Cursillo Movement, Twelfth Region, from 1990 to 1997. He is the honorary Conventual Chaplain of the Federal Association of the Sovereign Military Order of Malta, the Grand Prior of the North Central Lieutenancy of the United States for the Equestrian Order of the Holy Sepulchre of Jerusalem, and a member of the Council of Kohl McKornick Early Childhood Teaching Awards.

Since 1988 he has been a member of the Council of Administration of the Oblate Media at Belleville, Illinois. He is also a member of the American Catholic Philosophical Association, of the American Society of Missiologists, and of the Catholic Commission on Intellectual and Cultural Affairs.

At the Sixth General Congregation of the recent American Synod (Thursday 20 November 1997), he spoke on the theme, "A Comparison of Cultures."

Created and proclaimed Cardinal by John Paul II in the consistory of 21 February 1998, of the Title of St. Bartholemew on Tiberina Island.

Curial Membership:
- Divine Worship and Sacraments, Institutes of Consecrated Life and Societies of Apostolic Life, Evangelization of Peoples, Oriental Churches (congregations)
- *Cor Unum,* Culture (councils)
- Cultural Heritage (commission)
- *Vox Clara* (committee)
- Ordinary Council of the General Secretariat of the Synod of Bishops
- Special Council for America of the General Secretariat of the Synod of Bishops

Introduction

George Cardinal Pell

Cardinal Ratzinger in the preface to his 1999 work called *The Spirit of the Liturgy*, claimed that in 1918 at the conclusion of the First World War, when the distinguished German theologian Romano Guardini wrote the first *The Spirit of the Liturgy* which began the Liturgical Movement in Germany, the Roman liturgy was then rather like a fresco, which had been preserved from damage but was almost completely overlaid with whitewash. That fresco was laid bare by the Liturgical Movement and especially by the Second Vatican Council. In the years since then, Cardinal Ratzinger went on to explain that the fresco had been endangered by climatic conditions as well as by various restorations and reconstructions. So much so that the liturgy itself, he believed, was threatened with destruction. Steps had to be taken to stop those damaging influences. He then wrote his own small booklet using the same title as Guardini's, not to involve himself with scholarly discussion and research, but to work toward a renewal of the faith and of "the right way to give the faith its central form of expression in the liturgy."[1]

While there are considerable differences of nationality, professional interests, backgrounds and even of theological orientation among the three cardinals writing in this volume all of them would belong to the same broad category of Church thinkers as Cardinal Ratzinger and are equally dedicated to preserving and developing "the right way to give the faith its central form of expression in the liturgy."

Cardinal Francis Arinze is a Nigerian archbishop, who has worked in the Vatican for many years and has been Prefect of the Sacred Congregation for Divine Worship and the Discipline of the Sacraments since 2002. His talk was originally given to the seminar held in Rome for newly appointed bishops on September 17, 2004.

Not surprisingly he dealt more with the role of the bishop and to some extent that of the priest in the celebration of the liturgy than the ways the faithful might participate. Equally unsurprising was the fact that he began by restating that basic principle which is crucial for any Catholic understanding: It is Christ himself who is at the heart of our sacred Liturgy. It is Christ who "instituted the Church and sent her to preach His Good News and celebrate His sacred mysteries for the glory of God and the sanctification of humankind."[2] It is especially through the celebration of the Eucharist that the fruits of Jesus' unique passion, death, resurrection and ascension are bequeathed to us for the glory of God and to make men and women holy through right living, prayer and service.

The Cardinal Prefect points out that each diocesan bishop is the high priest of his flock, where his offices as teacher and shepherd are directed toward the sanctification of his people. His role as chief celebrant of the diocese is not a question of pride or honor, but of theological and ecclesiological truth. This important work of service is a duty.

As the moderator, promoter and guardian of the whole liturgical life of the diocese, the bishop must not only strive to inspire his priests and people toward a proper understanding of their different roles in a fruitful participation in the liturgy, but he must also explain and defend those sacramental understandings which are necessary for spiritual vitality.

Cardinal Arinze has a small but beautiful section on the importance of each cathedral church, which is "the most visible manifestation of the universal Church" in any diocese and where the liturgical celebrations should be models of prayer and excellence.

In the two archdioceses where I have been called to serve, I have been blessed with beautiful Neo-Gothic buildings constructed on a grand scale, with well-established traditions of faithful worship and liturgical propriety and each Cathedral possessing wonderful choirs. It was one of my proudest liturgical moments in Melbourne when a visiting nun from Papua New Guinea, who had attended our overflow midnight Mass for Christmas, told her companions afterward that she had thought she was in Heaven.

Cardinal Arinze concludes with a small section on inculturation, which "should be normal in evangelization," by remarking on

the considerable variety of approaches possible even among good bishops and warns against too frequent and unapproved changes, often the fruit of a celebrant's idiosyncrasy and fertile imagination!

Cardinal Jorge A. Medina Estévez had been archbishop of Valparaiso, in Chile until he was transferred to the Congregation for Divine Worship in 1996 where he remained as Cardinal Arinze's immediate predecessor until 2002. His time as Cardinal Prefect was important for liturgical reform generally and especially in the English-speaking world. The promulgation of *Liturgiam Autenticam* in March, 2001 "On the Use of Vernacular Languages in the Publication of the Books of the Roman Liturgy" will always remain an important landmark in the history of the implementation of liturgical reform after the Second Vatican Council and Cardinal Medina's leadership and courage were indispensable to its production. As a result of this, the English-speaking bishops around the world continued with the reform of ICEL (The International Commission on English in the Liturgy) which embarked on the long process of translating into English the revised *Roman Missal* (editio typica tertia). Cardinal Medina also oversaw the creation of the *Vox Clara* Committee, an international committee of cardinals, archbishops and bishops to advise the Congregation on this translation work. That the identity of these advisers on this important project is public knowledge represents something of a breakthrough in Vatican procedures and could be a useful precedent, perhaps even for other Congregations.

The Cardinal's article was published in *L'Osservatore Romano* of September 1, 2004, and is a typically rigorous theological evaluation of the notion of participating in the Sacred Liturgy.

He draws on the Conciliar documents and later official teachings to restate the basic Catholic understanding of the necessary and irreplaceable ministerial role of bishops and priests in the liturgical celebrations of the Church, which is "the sacrament of unity," as well as stressing the traditional teaching on the common priesthood of the faithful and their active, participatory roles in the communal celebrations of the liturgy. Central to all this is the official teaching that the liturgy is an exercise of the priestly office of Jesus Christ.

He then proceeds to a systematic examination of the type of participation urged by the Second Vatican Council, i.e., fully aware, actively engaged and enriched, which must be the consequence of

proper dispositions and of cooperation with heaven by grace. These inner dispositions correspond fundamentally to the theological virtues of faith, hope and love.

We cannot approach the reality of our unseen God of love without the virtue of faith, which recognizes God's power to transform the human and material signs we use in the sacraments. The Eucharistic liturgy cannot exist outside the light of faith and without a spirit of faith. Because of this faith in Christ, the only Son of God, liturgical celebrations cannot be reduced to the level of a gymnastic or folklore display. Only faith enables us, through prayer and worship, to participate in the eternal plan of salvation through the sacraments.

So too the ordained minister of the sacraments is neither an actor, nor an official, but an office holder who must be worthy, attentive and devout, a "believer in love with the ineffable presence of the One who cannot be seen."

Against the standards of much conventional practice throughout the English-speaking world Cardinal Medina bluntly reasserts the necessity of the state of grace for the sacraments. While the situation is further clouded by serious differences and uncertainties about what constitutes a mortal or death-bearing sin, and we are often urged "to come as we are," those in a state of mortal sin and without any desire for conversion are not truly participating, he asserts.

He does not believe that those without the proper interior dispositions should be excluded or discouraged from attending, because their presence might stir them to conversion, but neither does he believe that public sinners should play any official part in sacramental celebrations for fear of provoking scandals. As always prudence and sensitivity are needed as we struggle to apply appropriate safeguards to the sacraments.

He lists the various responsibilities of lectors, acolytes, extraordinary ministers and musicians such as the schola cantorum. So too the master of ceremonies is commended for his particular contribution, while in conclusion there is an eloquent section on the vertical dimension of the liturgy; the ascendant dimension of praise for our Creator and Redeemer and the descendant dimension where salvation reaches human beings through sanctifying grace and other godly blessings.

Cardinal Francis George, OMI, the Archbishop of Chicago, needs no introduction to American readers. An Oblate of Mary Immaculate, he has a professional background in philosophy as well as theology and has a crucial role in liturgical renewal today, as a member of ICEL, *Vox Clara* and the Congregation for Divine Worship. His paper is on the philosophical and anthropological areas of liturgical reform and was given to celebrate the fortieth anniversary of the Second Vatican Council Constitution on the Sacred Liturgy *Sacrosanctum Concilium*. His presentation is guided by two questions: a) who is the subject of the liturgy and b) how does that subject participate in the liturgy?

His thesis is that a lot of work has been done in liturgical theology but not enough has been done in the fields of philosophy, epistemology and cultural anthropology to chart our way from the naïve innocence of forty years ago to the pastoral shrewdness required today for an effective deepening and renewal of the liturgy.

Today some of the opponents of the new English translation of the Roman Missal are stressing the importance of continuity and highlighting the disturbance to the faithful when traditional patterns of praying are disturbed.

There is considerable truth in these claims and it will be difficult to establish consensus on some items of translation such as accuracy, orthodoxy, proclaimability because they are weighted differently by different schools of thought. But the translation changes now envisaged for the English of the Roman Missal are minor when compared with the downgrading of liturgical devotions, the introduction of the vernacular and the reworking of our sacramental symbolism to bring it closer to the style of Lutheranism and Anglicanism immediately after Vatican II.

The liturgical reformers after Vatican II were not overly concerned about disturbing long established patterns of devotion, and changes such as those just enumerated were earthquakes. In other words the whitewash which overlaid the tradition was often removed roughly. This is not to deny the significant gains that have been made. It implies no claim that many wish to return to the Tridentine Mass in Latin, because most do not. But the changes have been imperfect and have come at considerable cost.

Cardinal George commends the *Catechism of the Catholic Church* for the magisterial development of doctrine in its description of the liturgy as the work of the Trinity (CCC, 1136–1144); the Father, Son and Holy Spirit are the primary actors in the liturgy. Then come the heavenly powers, all creation, biblical saints, the martyrs, the all-holy Mother of God and the great multitude of the elect, who all accompany the celebrant and community. The earthly liturgy is a heavenly liturgy of the Body of Christ extending through space and time.

These rich and wide perspectives stand in strong contrast with some impoverished notions of the People of God, which have slipped into our consciousness to eliminate or weaken the vertical or Godly dimension of the sacraments, so that some liturgies are reduced to a localized, horizontal levelling, communities celebrating themselves, with little emphasis on prayer and interior worship.

If, for example, the role of the Holy Spirit is ignored, it is much easier to envisage the Eucharist as a memorial tableau, a recreation of the Last Supper rather than a representation in unbloody form of the unique sacrifice of Calvary.

Perhaps Cardinal George's most controversial claims are that the roots of the post-conciliar liturgical reforms are to be found in the Enlightenment, with both positive, e.g., noble simplicity, and negative consequences.

Therefore, reason was exalted at the expense of perception, imagination and intuition, so contributing to the profound secularization of the West today. The Enlightenment encouraged worship because it helped develop moral virtue. Thus moral instruction, not the worship of our unseen God, was seen as the central point of Church services.

The Enlightenment also provoked the reaction of the Romantics, producing new movements in art, literature, architecture. There were considerable benefits to the Church such as the Neo-Gothic movement in architecture and art but losses also. Cardinal George feels that much of the liturgical polarization today is between rationalist and romantic positions, while there are few people with the tools necessary to move beyond the impasse. According to the Cardinal while the Council highly recommended participation in the liturgy, its emphasis was too rationalistic, on verbal response and physical gesture, while the sacramental, internal and invisible dimension

of the liturgy was not elaborated. We need a better rationale for and a more expanded endorsement of prayerful, sacred silence.

In conclusion, Cardinal George urges that the liturgy should be ceremonious, formal and repetitive; in other words predictable and familiar. Social anthropology, he claims, does not justify any claim that simplicity in ritual form is more effective than complexity, or that a sign which is immediately intelligible will be more effective than a multifaceted symbol.

These claims are heresy for many older middle class churchgoers, active in liturgy committees and attached to many of the "new" ways. But we cannot automatically conclude from that that these insights are mistaken.

The three papers in this volume are all urging us to consider more deeply what forms of participation in the liturgy should be encouraged; what elements should be taken from the cultures which surround us, what elements should be developed or emphasized from within our own liturgical tradition. In other words all the Cardinals touch on the problematic of inculturation in different ways. Cardinal Arinze writes briefly, realistically and perhaps a trifle sceptically; Cardinal Medina's piece is a vigorous defence of the tradition; while Cardinal George attempts to identify the place of the reforms in the evolving cultural patterns of the English-speaking world.

The explicit discussion and endorsement of inculturation at the Second Vatican Council[3] was an innovation in Conciliar history, although the story of all the Ecumenical Councils details an unfinished dialogue between the Church with her continuing traditions and the societies which she was inhabiting. Many of the actual liturgical changes in the Latin rite were not spelled out in the Council documents but developed later; many of them under the broad heading of the inculturation of the liturgy, and some of these more explicitly under the narrow heading of *aggiornamento*, or bringing things up to date.

Here we have to confront a Conciliar deficiency, a lack of clarity and definition, which was first spelled out dramatically by Karl Barth the Protestant theologian writing in 1966 to Pope Paul VI. "What does *aggiornamento* mean? Accommodation to what?" he enquired.[4] The question remained unanswered for a long time until the unexpected losses in the Western World which followed the

Council, quite the opposite of what young priests then (like myself) expected, provoked a rethinking and reworking of the problematic.

The subsequent travails of the Church in the Western world have considerably purified the naïve human optimism which was such a strong current at the Second Vatican Council into something closer to realism and the theological virtue of hope.

To my mind, in any discussion of inculturation in the English-speaking worlds of today a number of understandings are vital to any accurate appreciation of the task before us.

1. Everywhere in the English-speaking world Catholics are a minority and regularly worshipping Catholics are an even smaller group. Ireland is the exception in both cases.

2. Nowhere in the English-speaking world do Catholics represent the dominant cultural group. While in some places we are a significant participant in the public dialogue, this influence often does not even parallel our numerical percentage of the population. Probably the only exception to this is Catholic life in the United States and even here within the Catholic community we have a variety of competing voices.

3. While we are under pressure in the culture wars at an intellectual level, these pressures are greater at the level of popular culture, where the worlds of advertising and mass entertainment are regularly corrosive of genuine religious and spiritual values. One has only to think of popular magazines, especially for teenagers, television, videos, DVDs, without mentioning the flood of pornography on the internet.

4. It is these hostile forces, more than our own mistakes which are promoting the steady decline in regular worship which is occurring in many places, not everywhere, but certainly in many parts of Australia. This decline in regular worship runs in parallel with a declining number of diocesan priests, the collapse and disappearance of some religious orders and the recruitment difficulties in many dioceses in attracting seminarians to prepare for the priesthood.

In other words, in many sections of Catholic life today we have what Professor Eamon Duffy, the distinguished medieval historian

and president of Magdalene College at Cambridge University, has described as "an all embracing erosion of meaning and certainty, the plight of modernity which none of us altogether escapes."[5] The Catholic Church still has many strengths and our liturgy and especially the sacraments continue to contribute to this strength. By itself no liturgical program, no matter how profound, spiritual and appropriate culturally to its congregation, could have succeeded in reversing this process. There has been too much damage to marriage, family, school and parish. But a renewed liturgy can help strengthen all these agencies and institutions.

The concept of inculturation has brought notable gains, the most significant of which is the movement of the liturgy from Latin into the vernacular. This has brought important pastoral advantages especially with young people and while it might not be universally popular it has the overwhelming majority support of Catholics, whether they practice regularly or infrequently. However, such gains have been bought at some cost. The concept of inculturation has been used in ways, often unwittingly, to allow the surrounding society, sometimes secular, sometimes superstitious in a New Age way, and sometimes merely reflecting some less desirable aspects of mass culture, e.g. hedonism, to enter into our liturgy, especially our music. So the uninitiated came to believe that they had a right to entertainment and novelty, should certainly be comforted and challenged rarely, if at all.

The Enlightenment and the Romantic movement have influenced the liturgy in conflicting ways but the cultural influences on the liturgy have been considerably wider than these forces. Within the Christian tradition the liturgical forms of Lutheranism and Anglicanism were also quietly significant, even if this has been rarely acknowledged publicly. On a wider front the forces at work in mass entertainment both deter young people from participating in the liturgy or encourage false understandings.

While we are all aware of the well-known saying of Prosper of Aquitaine *"Lex Orandi Lex Credendi,"* the way we pray can also be heavily influenced by the world around us and this can spill over into confusion at the doctrinal level. There is even a danger that God himself can be subtly downgraded. The movement in some quarters to replace the terminology of Father, Son and Holy Spirit with Creator, Redeemer and Sanctifier can easily encourage a slide toward

deism rather than encouraging an explicit belief in a personal and loving God.[6] So too a proper understanding of the role of the Holy Spirit in the liturgy which is conveyed by a sense of the importance of prayerful celebration, the need for reverence, and the obligation for personal worthiness or at least repentance can start to evaporate into a search for entertainment or personal therapy, for psychological healing.[7] This can lead to a collapse in the understanding of the liturgy as ritual, and a total lack of comprehension that the Eucharist is a work of divine artistry, which expresses at the one time both the concerns of today and the Passover of Jesus; the call of eternity, the Paschal Banquet to come at the end of time and the realities for good or ill of the here and now.[8]

To combat these misunderstandings one can only agree with Cardinal George that a more profound understanding of participation is needed. In fact the translation of *participato actuosa* as "active participation" is not entirely adequate. A secondary meaning of *actuosa* is effective and of course activity need not only be external. In the liturgy participation must be internal and spiritual and requires prayerful silence and listening.[9]

In his *Ad Limina* address to the Bishops from the North Western areas of the United States in 1998 John Paul II spoke beautifully about active participation. "Full participation" he said "does not mean that everyone does everything . . . the liturgy, like the Church is intended to be hierarchical and polyphonic." He then continued, "In a culture which neither favors nor fosters meditative quiet, the art of interior listening is learned only with difficulty. Here we see how the liturgy, though it must always be properly inculturated, must also be counter cultural." The Roman rite, he said, has a distinctive balance "between a spareness and richness of emotion; it feeds the heart and the mind, the body and the soul."[10]

The hymn singing powers of Catholics have often been compared unfavorably with those of the Protestants. As well as that and despite the good work of Pope Saint Gregory the Great, there is a long tradition of Christian writers such as Saint Jerome, Saint Augustine and even Saint Thomas Aquinas who have been quite sceptical about the spiritual value of hymn singing. Aquinas justified the singing of hymns so that "the minds of the weak are more effectively summoned to piety."[11]

From my own years as a young layman and then a priest and a bishop I have fond memories of deeply devotional hymn singing. As a schoolboy I remember over 300 boarders in the College Chapel bringing down the roof singing lustily together "Faith of Our Fathers" or "We Stand for God" and there was a considerable amount of faith and genuine devotion as well as a strong tribal pride and sense of belonging. Men and women prefer different sorts of hymns, but there are certainly hymns which they will sing happily together, boys and girls, men and women of every age. I remember with the fondest memories the traditional Compline sung at the end of the day in Latin in our seminary and recall deeply moving moments of silent prayer in my Cathedrals as brilliant choirs executed some of the gems of the Catholic polyphonic tradition, which must rank among the high points of Western cultural achievement. I have different memories of enhanced participation in small country churches with wonderful community singing at Mass; as well as another congregation which refused to sing. I suggested as a Lenten Penance that they all take out their hymnbooks and hold them up, even if they still chose not to participate through singing! They still refused to sing.

To enhance effective participation children today should be exposed to a wide repertoire of Church hymns, which need not be only contemporary compositions, anymore than they need to be written 50 or a 100 years ago. In both the old and new hymns there are some which will regularly be sung with faith and devotion and which express good sound theology. Children will happily sing some of the old hymns if they are taught and there should be no excessive strictures against somewhat sentimental and theologically unsophisticated hymns. Not every one needs to follow the dryer, middle class sensibilities on these issues, provided the message of the hymns is orthodox, and the music is not agitated or sensual, leading us to a celebration of the profane not the sacred.

Experience as a bishop also revealed to me an iron law which rules during the celebration of Confirmation. The fewer the number of people in the congregation who know a hymn the more verses will be sung by the Confirmation choir which has been especially prepared for the occasion!

There are many types of hymn singing, completely at one with the Church's doctrines and liturgical tradition which can and do enhance prayerful participation.

A final word about the obligation to participate in regular worship. In Australia we have many Catholic schools, largely financed by government funding. In these schools we can have many non-Catholics and of the Catholics more than seventy-five percent might not worship regularly. Such a mixed community obviously provides a difficult audience for any talk about the obligation to worship. However it is an unfortunate departure from Catholic tradition if we do not explain sensitively, but with some regularity, the obligation we have to worship the one true God in Christ the Redeemer, his only Son. How we explain this obligation to our regular churchgoers, as well as to Catholics who only worship occasionally, depends on the level of theological understanding and on the age and disposition of the listeners. But if it is never pointed out to believers that there is an obligation to participate regularly at the Eucharist, to confess our sins regularly in the sacrament of penance and to receive the other Sacraments, then we are departing from New Testament practice as well as the tradition of the Church.

It also has the consequence of reducing the status of God himself and Christ his Son to something like that of a distant relative, of whom we think well, but who only needs to be visited once or twice a year, perhaps at Christmas and Easter. The notions of duty and obligation, especially in religion, are counter-cultural, but they are essential in the Christian tradition.

Conclusion

As long ago as 1965 in a letter to Pope Paul VI, Romano Guardini explained beautifully what is at the heart of appropriate Christian inculturation. "What can convince modern people is not a historical or a psychological or a continually ever-modernizing Christianity, but only the unrestricted and uninterrupted message of revelation."[12]

A proper participation in the liturgy does not seek to exclude or dull the call to repent and believe. Neither does it seek to remove the tension between the followers of Christ and "the world, the flesh and the devil." Genuine participation must be a prayerful seeking

of the Spirit, an interior activity as much as it is external and communitarian; something which feeds heart and mind, body and soul.

Above all participation must be Christ-centred. In John's gospel we read that Jesus said, "I am the true vine, and my father is the vine dresser . . . and every branch that does bear fruit he prunes to make it bear even more."[13]

So may it be in the liturgy.

---

1. Cardinal Joseph Ratzinger, *The Spirit of the Liturgy* (San Francisco: Ignatius Press, 2000), pp. 7–8.

2. *Sacrosanctum Concilium*, 5–6.

3. *Sacrosanctum Concilium*, 33–40.

4. Quoted in Tracey Rowland, *Culture and the Thomist Tradition after Vatican II* (London and New York: Routledge, 2003), p. 19.

5. Eamon Duffy, *Faith of Our Fathers: Reflections on Catholic Tradition* (London, New York: Continuum, 2004), p. 178.

6. M. Francis Mannion, *Masterworks of God: Essays in Liturgical Theory and Practice* (Chicago: Hillenbrand Books, 2004), p. 5.

7. M. Francis Mannion, ibid., p. 108.

8. M. Francis Mannion, ibid., pp. 16–18, 80–83.

9. R. J. Schuler, "Misunderstanding of *Actuosa Participatio*," *Sacred Music*, 122 (3) (Fall 1995), 5. The writings of Cardinal Ratzinger are also useful here. See *The Feast of Faith* (San Francisco: Ignatius Press, 1986), pp. 68–75.

10. Pope John Paul II, *Origins*, 28 (5/11/1998), pp. 378–380.

11. Cardinal Joseph Ratzinger, *Feast of Faith*, pp. 103–113.

12. Quoted in Tracey Rowland, *Culture and the Thomist Tradition after Vatican II*, p. 22.

13. John 15:1–2.

Active Participation in the Sacred Liturgy

Francis Cardinal Arinze

In issuing its first document, *Sacrosanctum Concilium* (henceforth SC) more than 40 years ago, one of the major concerns of the Second Vatican Council was that all the faithful take as full a part as possible in liturgical celebrations. It is therefore right that this 2004 annual Conference of the Society for Catholic Liturgy has taken as its major theme the revisiting of active participation in the sacred liturgy.
I thank you for inviting me to propose some reflections to this august assembly on this important topic.

We shall begin by reviewing what the Council said and then reflecting on the basis for this active participation and how our earthly liturgy reflects the heavenly one. There have been exaggerations in the understanding and practice of active participation. It therefore pays to articulate its genuine aims, its manifestations and its grades. A consideration of the importance of interior participation, silence and contemplation will bring these reflections to an end.

1. Active Participation: The Council Decree

A leitmotiv that runs through SC is active participation in liturgical celebrations. "Mother church earnestly desires that all the faithful be led to that full, conscious and active participation in liturgical celebrations which is demanded by the very nature of the liturgy" (SC, 14). The Council goes on to say that this is the consideration to be given priority in the liturgical renewal. It states: "In the restoration and promotion of the sacred liturgy, this full and active participation by all the people is the aim to be considered before all else; for it is the primary and indispensable source from which the faithful are to derive the true Christian spirit" (SC, 14). SC continues to recall the

importance of such participation, for example, in articles 19, 26, 27, 30, 31, 50 and 55.

Active participation is necessary because every liturgical celebration is an action of Christ the priest and of his Body the Church. The Council therefore refers to the importance of all the faithful being duly involved in many parts of SC, like when it treats liturgical formation of clergy and people, adaptation and inculturation, communitarian celebrations, language, more abundant readings from Holy Scripture, the Mass, the sacraments, the Liturgy of the Hours, the liturgical year, and sacred music and art. All is presented in the light of a more conscious and devoted participation, and therefore of the need for the proper liturgical formation of priests and of due catechesis of the lay faithful.

"Liturgical services," says the Council, "are not private functions, but are celebrations of the Church, which is the 'sacrament of unity,' namely, a holy people united and organized under their Bishops" (SC, 26; cf. also CIC, 899.2). For this reason the Council decrees that communal celebrations which involve the active participation of the faithful are to be preferred to celebrations that are individual and quasi-private (SC, 27). Moreover due observance of roles is to be the norm: "In liturgical celebrations, whether as a minister or as one of the faithful, each person should perform his role by doing solely and totally what the nature of things and liturgical norms require of him" (SC, 28).

The Council does not want the people of God to be deprived of this participation which is variously described as full, active, conscious, interior, exterior and sacramental (cf. SC, 19l, 30).

2. Basis for Active Participation

Baptism is the major basis for the active participation of all the faithful of Christ in liturgical celebrations. By this fundamental sacrament of Christian initiation the Christian people are made "a chosen race, a royal priesthood, a holy nation, a purchased people" (1 Peter 2:9; cf. 2:4–5). By their share in the common priesthood, all the baptized are empowered to take part in Christian worship. At Holy Mass, for example, while the ordained priest, acting in the person of Christ, brings about the Eucharistic Sacrifice and offers it to God in the name

of all the people, the faithful for their part join in the offering of the Eucharist by virtue of their royal priesthood (cf. *Lumen gentium*, 10). Therefore active participation by all the faithful is not a concession but a right founded on Baptism.

There is a difference in how people take part in the liturgy. It is true that all liturgical celebrations pertain to the whole of the Church, manifest it and have effects on it. But the Council reminds us that these celebrations "concern individual members of the Church in different ways, according to the diversity of Holy Orders, functions and degrees of participation" (SC, 26).

At the general level of participation are all the baptized. The liturgical assembly is the community of the baptized who "by regeneration and the anointing of the Holy Spirit are consecrated into a spiritual house and a holy priesthood. Thus through all those works befitting Christian people they can offer spiritual sacrifices and proclaim the power of him who has called them out of darkness into his marvelous light (cf. 1 Peter 2:4–10)" (*Lumen gentium*, 120; *Catechism of the Catholic Church*, 1141).

But in the Church "the members do not all have the same function" (Romans 12:4). Ordained priests are called by God, in and through the Church, to a special service of the Christian community. They are consecrated by the sacrament of Holy Orders by which the Holy Spirit enables them to act in the person of Christ the head, for the service of all the members of the Church. The ministerial priest is at the height of his service at the Eucharistic celebration. The Bishop is the Chief Priest in his diocese. And deacons are assigned special ministries close to the Bishop and the priest.

There is another title to participation in the sacred liturgy which has to be mentioned. In order to assist the work of the common priesthood of the faithful other particular ministries also exist. These are not consecrated by the sacrament of Holy Orders. Rather their functions are determined by the Bishops, in accord with liturgical traditions and pastoral needs. Examples are servers, lectors, commentators and members of the choir. "These also exercise a genuine liturgical ministry" (SC, 29; cf. also CCC, 1143).

When the needs of the Church require it and the ordained ministers are lacking, lay members of Christ's faithful can be appointed to supply for certain liturgical offices according to the norm of law.

Examples are extraordinary ministers of Holy Communion (cf. Congregation for Divine Worship and the Discipline of the Sacraments: *Redemptionis Sacramentum*, 146–160).

When therefore we speak of active participation in liturgical celebrations, we are dealing with a consequence that has sacramental basis in Baptism and Holy Orders and also liturgical traditions proven through time.

3. The Earthly Liturgy Reflects the Heavenly One

A major consideration that underlines the importance of active participation in the sacred liturgy is the relationship between earth and heaven in the public worship of the Church.

The divine life is that of love, glory and freedom. The human being, created in God's image, and redeemed by Christ, is given by God the possibility of participating in the divine life. This redemptive grace reaches people especially through the sacraments when celebrated, participated in, and faithfully lived out.

It is the sacred liturgy that in a special way makes possible this participation in the divine life. Liturgical celebration postulates, makes possible and increases the indwelling of the Blessed Trinity in Christ's faithful so that they can the more give glory to the Father, through the Son, in the unity of the Holy Spirit.

Liturgical participation here below on earth tends toward the future, toward heaven. As the Second Vatican Council puts it, "Our union with the Church in heaven is put into effect in the noblest manner when with common rejoicing we celebrate together the praise of the vine majesty. . . . Such is especially the case in the sacred liturgy, where the power of the Holy Spirit acts upon us through sacramental signs. Celebrating the Eucharistic sacrifice, therefore, we are most closely united to the worshiping Church in heaven as we join with and venerate the memory first of all of the glorious ever-Virgin Mary, of Blessed Joseph and the blessed apostles and martyrs, and of all the saints" (*Lumen gentium*, 50).

The CCC states the same comforting truth: "By the Eucharistic celebration we already unite ourselves with the heavenly liturgy and anticipate eternal life, when God will be all in all" (CCC, 1326).

Pope John Paul II returns to the same theme: "The Eucharist is truly a glimpse of heaven appearing on earth. It is a glorious ray of the heavenly Jerusalem which pierces the clouds of our history and lights up our journey" (*Ecclesia de Eucharistia*, 19).

When, therefore, we talk of active participation in the sacred liturgy, it is a matter of the part that the baptized have in the celebration here on earth which is related to the heavenly liturgy. The liturgical participation will find its eventual conclusion at the end of our earthly sojourn for each of us, and at the end of the world for the entire Church. Who does not appreciate the importance of such participation? Are we not thereby striving to contribute our part so that the will of God may be done on earth as it is done in heaven? "Where God's will is done," says Cardinal Ratzinger, "there is heaven, and earth becomes heaven. Surrendering ourselves to the action of God, so that we in our turn may cooperate with him—that is what begins in the liturgy and is meant to unfold further beyond it" (Joseph Ratzinger, *The Spirit of the Liturgy*, San Francisco: Ignatius Press, 2000, p. 176).

4. Exaggerations on Active Participation

The liturgical movement did very good service for many decades in preparing the Church for that liturgical renewal which first appeared officially in the Easter Vigil as restored by Pope Pius XII in 1952. The greatest fruit of the liturgical movement was the liturgical renewal as decreed by the Second Vatican Council. One major area where the leaders of the liturgical movement paid attention was that the lay faithful become less passive at liturgical celebrations, especially at Holy Mass. Although the Church never said so, from the Council of Trent (1545–1563) liturgical celebrations looked more and more like actions of the clergy in which the laity were present. The Second Vatican Council made a big and successful effort to redress that impression.

It is not a surprise that soon after this Council some people began to exaggerate to the extreme of activism in liturgical participation. They seemed to be pushing an unwritten agenda of active participation at all costs, in all sorts of ways, by everyone and in all parts of the liturgy if possible. Sometimes this led to noisy celebrations in which the roles of ordained priests and the lay faithful who have the royal

priesthood were confused. Silence and times for meditative listening were apparently not considered important. Activism, or the effort to get everyone to be doing something active all the time, was sponsored as if it were what the Second Vatican Council desired (cf. Congregation for Divine Worship and the Discipline of the Sacraments: *Redemptionis Sacramentum*, 40).

Sometimes such tendencies appeared in choirs dominating the celebrations, occupying positions that distract the congregation and edging out the priest celebrant to a role of secondary importance. At other times, activism appears in endless commentaries where the speaker is probably unconsciously projecting self-image and is doing his or her best not to allow the priest or the people to have a quiet moment. A recent craze for so-called active participation is the idea that there must be dance at a solemn Mass. I have seen a Mass where some misguided person arranged a dance for entry, another for *Gloria in Excelsis Deo,* another for the Gospel, one for the offertory, one for *Sanctus,* one for thanksgiving after Communion and a final exhibition for exit! This dance operator forgot to tell us whether people come to Sunday Mass in order to watch dances, whether there is no parish hall for dances after Mass, and whether the Latin Mass liturgy had the tradition of dance. Why must the people of God be afflicted with so many distractions just when they come to adore God on Sunday?

All this leads us to state that while the Second Vatican Council ordered fuller, more conscious, and active participation in the liturgy, it is of vital importance that we accept that the liturgy is primarily something that Christ does, not something that we put together. It is something that we receive, not something that we invent. It is a celebration of the mysteries of Christ in which we are allowed to take part as members of the Church. "True liturgical education cannot consist in learning and experimenting with external activities. Instead one must be led toward the essential *action* that makes the liturgy what it is, toward the transforming power of God, who wants, through what happens in the liturgy, to transform us and the world" (J. Ratzinger, *op. cit.*, p. 175).

Let us now go into greater detail by examining the aims of active participation and mentioning some of its manifestations, exterior and interior.

5. The Aim of Liturgical Participation

It is important that we have before our eyes the aim of participation in the sacred liturgy.

The sacred liturgy is celebrated in order to give praise to God and promote the sanctification of people. It is a celebration of the mysteries of Christ the Redeemer. The Son of God, by his suffering, death and resurrection, has freed us from the power of Satan (cf. Acts 26:18) and from death and brought us into the kingdom of his Father. The highest point of the liturgy is the Eucharistic celebration. "As often as the sacrifice of the cross in which 'Christ, our Passover, has been sacrificed '(1 Corinthians 5:7) is celebrated on the altar, the work of our redemption is carried on" (*Lumen gentium*, 3).

It is important that all the faithful share in the celebration of these saving mysteries of Christ. Baptism opens the door. By it people "are plunged into the paschal mystery of Christ" (SC, 6). In Confirmation they are strengthened by a more abundant outpouring of the Holy Spirit. In the other sacraments they are restored to God's grace, strengthened for their last journey, or given graces of state or the priesthood or the married life. In particular in the Holy Eucharist they take part at a sacramental re-presentation of the sacrifice of Calvary and are fed with the body and blood of the Lord. In other liturgical celebrations they are sanctified and enabled to be the voice of the Church at prayer.

The sacred liturgy is therefore "the summit toward which the activity of the Church is directed; at the same time it is the fountain from which all her power flows. . . . From the liturgy, therefore, and especially from the Eucharist, as from a fountain, grace is channeled into us; and the sanctification of people in Christ and the glorification of God, to which all other activities of the Church are directed as toward their goal, are most powerfully achieved" (SC, 10). We could not think of the Church without the liturgy.

Full, active and conscious participation enables the faithful of Christ to reap more abundant fruit from liturgical celebrations. It enables the salvific event of the celebration of the mysteries of Christ to exert more influence in them. It makes possible for them a deeper share in the divine life which Christ the Savior brought all humanity.

All this means that the better and deeper is the participation on the part of a person, the greater fruit will that person carry away from the liturgy. Let us examine several grades or possibilities.

6. Grades of Participation

The liturgical participation, state and involvement of a participant in a liturgical action do influence how much grace that person can receive.

Let us take as an example the following people taking part at a Eucharistic celebration: an atheist, a malefactor, a person of another religion other than Christian, a Christian in mortal sin, a Christian with attachment to venial sins, a fervent Christian, a saintly Christian, and a Christian mystic well advanced in a life of union with God.

Let us imagine that the fictitious people just named all come to Mass. And they mean sincerely to take part. They strive, according to their various states and capacities, to listen, to share with the assembly common postures like standing, sitting, or kneeling, and they try to understand and share what is going on. Only the four last named know that they can receive Holy Communion.

What is likely to be the result of their participation? In the final analysis, only God knows. But we can hazard the following possibilities. The defiant and unbelieving may show no visible change, but grace working secretly in them could arouse healthy curiosity, which can lead we know not where and how far. The Christian sinner might obtain at least the beginnings of the actual grace of repentance. The mediocre Christian could be led to more fervent commitment to the faith. The saintly Christian and the mystic could grow in their lives of union with God in ways beyond our observation.

None of this is automatic. Spiritual life and growth are primarily God's work. He it is who takes the initiative. But God who created us without our cooperation will not sanctify and save us without our cooperation. This is another way of saying that our commitment and degree of conscious and active participation in the sacred liturgy do influence the effects of these celebrations in us. Let us now examine some ways in which this participation can manifest itself.

7. Some External Manifestations of Active Participation

Sacrosanctum Concilium itself lists some of the external manifestations of active participation: acclamations, responses, psalmody, antiphons and songs, as well as actions, gestures and bodily attitudes (SC, 30). The Council goes further to say that "in the revision of liturgical books, it should be carefully provided that the rubrics take the role of the people into account" (SC, 31). This has been done in the revised rites these forty years.

All this is very healthy. Nobody should downplay the importance of these external manifestations. The human being is body and soul. Although interior dispositions are obviously more important, they do not undermine the importance of exterior manifestations, because these latter make visible, intensify and feed the interior requirements. It would be bad psychology and false angelism to ignore the importance of exterior manifestations.

Implied in all this is that liturgical celebrations should be devoted, faith-filled and artistically of high quality. Sacred music, quality of reading performance, altar equipment, sacred vestments and seating and kneeling provision for the congregation—each has its importance.

On the other hand, over-regimentation of the congregation by way of, for instance, unconditional and severe demanding of kneeling or standing when the approved rubrics do not say so, should be avoided. Unity in postures by the congregation is a good thing. All things being equal, it should take precedence over private inclination or arbitrary choice (cf. *General Instruction of the Roman Missal*, 42). But it is quite another matter when some parish or diocesan officials become rigid or dictatorial and make no concession whatsoever to personal piety, like a desire to receive Holy Communion on one's knees or the choice to kneel after returning to one's seat.

8. Interior Dispositions, Silence, and Contemplation

No matter how perfect the exterior manifestations of active participation may be, the interior dispositions are even more important.

SC recognizes this: "In order that the sacred liturgy may produce its full effect, it is necessary that the faithful come to it with proper dispositions, that their thoughts match their words, and that they cooperate with divine grace lest they receive it in vain (cf. 2 Corinthians 6:1)" (SC, 11).

Of fundamental requirement are the theological virtues of faith, hope and charity. Whoever is making progress in these basic attitudes of openness to God is making a better inner preparation for liturgical participation. And to these virtues should be added the virtue of religion and consequent piety which makes us devoted to God, who is our Father but also our Creator and Judge.

Listening is not a passive affair. It is an active openness to God's action in us. It makes us ready to receive the Word of God proclaimed in the liturgical assembly. It leads us to listen to the homily as it applies the sacred readings to the realities and challenges of life on earth today. Listening also includes reverent attention as the priest says or sings the prayers and the preface at Mass and recites the Eucharistic prayers. Listening moreover includes obedience to the directives given by the deacon or other authorized person in the worshipping assembly.

Silence has its place and importance as a help toward the promotion of the required interior dispositions. "At the proper times all should observe a reverent silence" (SC, 30). "For in the liturgy God speaks to his people and Christ is still proclaiming his Gospel" (SC, 33). The purpose of silence depends on the time it occurs in each part of a celebration.

Within the Act of Penitence at the beginning of Mass, and again after the invitation to prayer at Mass and other liturgical celebrations, a period of silence serves as a call to recollection. After the readings and the homily, a suitable pause can help people to meditate and interiorize what they have heard. After Holy Communion, silence serves to allow people to praise God and pray to him in their hearts (cf. *General Instruction of the Roman Missal*, 45).

A period of silence before liturgical celebrations is a help to recollection. It has, for example, been traditional in the Latin Missal to include in the appendix some prayers recommended to the priest before and after Mass. We human beings are often rather distracted by many things in life. We need a space between our daily activities and

our celebration of the sacred rites in order to help us cut out, or at least reduce, the noise of the world without.

It goes without saying that careful preparation for a liturgical celebration will spare the assembly from being distracted by nervous gestures or movements from the celebrant and other ministers. If organizers of theatrical exhibitions pay attention to details, much more is expected form all those who contribute to the celebration of the mysteries of Christ.

We live in an age of high technology and a quick-fix-it mentality. And that is good. But this propensity should not be allowed to do damage to a contemplative attitude in the liturgy. Every liturgical celebration should provide moments for silence, personal prayer and contemplative openness to God.

Respected officers and members of The Society for Catholic Liturgy, the Second Vatican Council was right in asking for a participation by all the faithful in the liturgy in a way that is full, conscious and active. The challenge for the whole Church is how that is to be promoted so that maximum spiritual fruit may be reaped.

May the Blessed Virgin Mary, Mother of Jesus and our Savior and Mother of the church, obtain for us the grace to do our part.

Commentary on the Instruction *Redemptionis Sacramentum:* Participating in the Sacred Liturgy

Jorge A. Cardinal Medina Estévez

Introduction

The notion of participation in the liturgy is based on doctrinal principles rooted in Catholic ecclesiology. If ecclesial activities, according to the Second Vatican Council (cf. *Lumen gentium,* 25; *Christus Dominus,* 12–16; *Presbyterorum Ordinis,* 4–6), revolve around the proclamation of the Word of God, the celebration of the liturgy and the action stemming from the pastoral administration of the People of God, it would be erroneous to imagine that it is only ordained minisgters who take an active part in it and that the participation of the faithful is exclusively passive. The program "give-receiving" does not exactly correspond to the profound nature of Catholic ecclesiology but is an excessive simplification of a far richer reality.

Several texts illustrate this point: "Liturgical services are not private functions but are celebrations of the Church which is 'the sacrament of unity,' namely, 'the holy people united and arranged under their Bishops.' Therefore, liturgical services pertain to the whole Body of the Church. They manifest it and have effects upon it. But they also touch individual members of the Church in different ways, depending on their orders, their role in the liturgical services and their actual participation in them" (*Sacrosanctum Concilium,* 26).

The logical conclusion of the previous assertions is that" "Rites which are meant to be celebrated in common, with the faithful present and actively participating, should as far as possible be celebrated in that way rather than by an individual and quasi-privately" (SC, 27).

And, more concretely, "In liturgical celebrations each person, minister of layman who has an office to perform, should carry out

all and only those parts which pertain to his office by the nature of the rite and norms of the liturgy" (SC, 28).

It is important to note that the Council's choice of vocabulary shows a preference for the term "celebration," which stresses the *ecclesial* and *community* dimensions of liturgical services. The new *Code of Canon Law* also makes frequent use of this word but does not exclude the term "administration" of the sacraments, which also conveys important theological concepts with a view to a correct understanding of the nature and efficacy of the sacraments.

It should surprise no one, therefore, that the word "celebration" has acquired special importance in liturgical catechesis and in the current vocabulary of both priests ad the faithful.

Let us continue our reflection, citing other texts of the Second Vatican Council: "The liturgy, then, is rightly seen as an exercise of the priestly office of Jesus Christ. It involves the presentation of man's sanctification under the guise of signs perceptible by the senses and its accomplishment in ways appropriate to each of these signs. In it full pubic worship is performed by the mystical body of Jesus Christ, that is, by the Head and his members" (SC, 7, 2).

"Christ, indeed, always associates the Church with himself in this great work in which God is perfectly glorified and men are sanctified. The Church is his beloved Bride who calls to her Lord, and through him offers worship to the eternal Father" (SC, 7, 1).

"From this it follows that every liturgical celebration, because it is an action of Christ the Priest and of his Body, which is the Church, is a sacred action surpassing all others. No other action of the Church can equal its efficacy by the same title and to the same degree" (SC, 7, 3).

After referring to various complementary doctrinal aspects in the Constitution *Sacrosanctum Concilium*, we should recall the Conciliar teaching on the common priesthood of the faithful. In returning to an ancient subject, it gives an excellent explanation of the basis for the participation of the faithful in liturgical celebrations. This text, from the Dogmatic Constitution on the Church *Lumen gentium*, is of capital importance. We cite it here: "Christ the Lord, high priest taken from among men (cf. Hebrews 5:1–5), made the new people 'a kingdom of priest to God, his Father' (Revelations 1:6; cf. 5:9–10). The baptized, by regeneration and the anointing of the Holy Spirit, are

consecrated to be a spiritual house and a holy priesthood, that through all the works of Christian men they may offer spiritual sacrifices and proclaim the perfection of him who has called them out of darkness into his marvelous light (cf. 1 Peter 2:4–10).

"Therefore, all the disciples of Christ, persevering in prayer and praising God (cf. Acts 2:42–47), should present themselves as a sacrifice, living, holy and pleasing to God (cf. Romans 12:1). They should answer to everyone who asks reason for the hope of an eternal life which is theirs (cf. 1 Peter 3:15). Though they differ essentially and not only in degree, the common priesthood of the faithful and the ministerial of hierarchical priesthood are nonetheless ordered one to another, each in its own proper way shares in the one priesthood of Christ.

"The ministerial priest, by the sacred power that he has, forms and rules the priestly people; in the person of Christ he effects the Eucharistic sacrifice and offers it to God in the name of all the people. The faithful indeed, by virtue of their royal priesthood, participate in the offering of the Eucharist. They exercise that priesthood, too, by the reception of the sacraments, prayer and thanksgiving, the witness of a holy life, abnegation and active charity" (*Lumen gentium*, 10).

Christian life, therefore, must be seen as a hymn of "praise to the glorious grace" of God (Ephesians 1:6, 12, 14), and offering of ourselves to God, a living and holy sacrifice, knowing that what pleases him is perfect (cf. Romans 12).

This praise acquires its value from our incorporation into Christ at the moment of our Baptism, and from the fact that the perfect praise of Christ on the Cross gives rise to our own praise or rather, in other words, our praise is incorporated into the praise of Christ precisely through the renewed presence of his Sacrifice, made once and for all (cf. Hebrews 727; 9:12, 28; 10:12, 14) on Calvary.

Thus, we can say in this regard that Christian life is a priestly life, a life consecrated to the glorification of God, or again, a "liturgical life"; it is not restricted solely to the celebration of liturgical worship in the strict sense but is also based on this worship and, living it as its summit (*Sacrosanctum Concilium*, 10), transpires in all our actions, including those that derive directly from temporal responsibilities or bear the hallmark of what is temporary or incomplete.

Participation

For a deeper knowledge of our topic, participation in the liturgy, it is of course vital to take these considerations into account. The most explicit text of the Second Vatican Council on the participation of the faithful in the liturgy says: "In order that the liturgy may be able to produce its full effects it is necessary that the faithful come to it with proper dispositions, that their minds be attuned to their voices, and that they cooperate with heavenly grace lest they receive it in vain. Pastors of souls must therefore realize that when the liturgy is celebrated, something more is required that the laws governing valid and lawful celebration. It is their duty also to ensure that the faithful take part fully aware of what they are doing, actively engaged in the rite and enriched by it" (*Sacrosanctum Concilium*, 11).

The three descriptions of participation used in this conciliar text are therefore: "fully aware," "actively engaged" and "enriched," but the text says that these three characteristics are something more than the mere observance of "proper dispositions" and cooperation "with heavenly grace."

Hence, the phrases: "come to it," "take part," "take part fully aware," "actively engaged" and "attuned" do not only merely concern external aspects but above all and primarily inter, spiritual dispositions. Were this not the case, the liturgical celebration would inevitably become a sort of performance or rather, a folklore display or an empty ritual and hence, a gymnastic or choreographic exercise!

The inner dispositions required for fruitful participation in the celebration of the liturgy correspond fundamentally to the theological virtues: faith, hope and charity. If it is true, as Saint Paul says three times, that "he who through faith is righteous shall live" (cf. Romans 1:17, Hebrews 10:38; Galatians 3:11), it is clear that the Eucharistic Liturgy, the summit of Christian life, cannot exist outside the light of faith or without a spirit of faith.

It is also true that Christian faith, the virtue proper to our condition as pilgrims, is necessarily accompanied by faith.

Faith shows us the meaning of our existence here on earth and the means we must use in this world to attain the definitive goal of our lives.

Hope, for its part, keenly aware of our weaknesses and the wounds left in our souls by sin, looks confidently at the final destination of our pilgrimage, certain of being able to reach it with God's help, the only thing that can introduce us into a "connatural" relationship with God, the source of being, salvation and the life of beatitude.

Faith and hope must of course lead to charity, whose inseparable objective is on the one hand God in himself, and on the other, through love of God, our neighbor. It is clear that it is a question of loving God with all our heart, all our strength and all our being, and at the same time loving our brothers and sisters in the deeply moving way that Saint Paul describes (cf. 1 Corinthians 13:1–13).

To the theological virtues, we can add yet another inner disposition, indispensable for a fruitful participation in the liturgy: the virtue of religion.

This phrase, "virtue of religion," suggests the deep respect and humble adoration of the One who is thrice Holy, whom se are not worthy even to approach (cf. Exodus 3:1–6; 1 Kings 19:9–13). We can say that the virtue of religion is, as it were, the "soul" of the liturgy; indeed, although we can never forget that God is our Father, he is nonetheless, a Father of immense majesty, the almighty Lord, the King of eternal glory.

Faith

To go more deeply into the various aspects of faith, let us now return to the theological virtue of faith. It is true that since the divine realities are part of the mystery of faith, access to the realities invisible to our fleshly eyes is barred to us except through faith (cf. Hebrews 11:1); nor can we reach the conviction without faith that everything we see comes from what we do not see (cf. Hebrews 11:3).

Indeed, it is faith that reveals what is invisible through what is visible, faith that transcends tangible experiences and gives us access to the mystery; lastly, it is precisely faith that allows us to perceive the effective meaning of the liturgical actions in the history of salvation, given that the liturgy is not an abstract construction unconnected with time.

It is a celebration firmly rooted in the interwoven events that constitute the fabric of the eternal plan f salvation, achieved as the

Father desired, as it was made manifest in the Incarnate Word and as it continues to be brought about in the Church through the action of the Holy Spirit.

Signs

Let us now address the specific question of liturgical signs and symbols. It can be said without any doubt that the *raison d'être* of the signs that mark the liturgy derives from human nature, considered both in its corporeal and spiritual dimensions, but it also derives from the mystery of the incarnation through which access to the invisible God becomes possible through the human reality of Jesus Christ.

In fact, just as Christ's humanity is the instrument for the saving action of the Word, so the liturgical signs contain and transmit God's saving power; through them. God's grace is communicated or intensified in all who have already received justification, divine adoption and incorporation in the Church.

Of course, comprehension of the liturgical signs is part and parcel of a conscious and fruitful participation in the liturgy. Yet even if, merely by their presence these signs exercise a pedagogical role for those who perceive them with a limited knowledge of their content, they nonetheless also demand the presence of a constant mystagogy and a formation based on liturgical catechesis that can enable both the faithful and ministers to progress in their knowledge of the mystery being celebrated.

The observation is particularly important with regard to a rite seldom celebrated, such as, for example, an ordination or the dedication of a new church. Nothing is more deleterious to the spiritual participation of the faithful in a liturgical celebration than an excessively hasty or distracted attitude in the celebrant or a mechanical approach to carrying out the liturgical actions.

Three words taken from a traditional prayer effectively sum up the attitude indispensable to every celebrant: "worthy," "attentive," "devout," for it is true that the celebrant himself is a sign. As a person who has been consecrated and an instrument of the action of the glorious Christ who plays the lead in sacramental actions, the ordained minister, and the members of the lay faithful delegated in accordance with the norms of law, must let the mystery being

celebrated shine out in such a way that the community can perceive that the above-mentioned minister is neither an actor on stage nor an official, but a believer in love with the ineffable presence of the One who cannot be seen with the eyes of the flesh but is more real than all that belongs to the world of the senses.

A worthy liturgical celebration must first be steeped in the beauty of the place in which it is celebrated and of the objects of worship used, even if this is a simple and essential beauty. This includes the cleanliness of the liturgical vestments and the quality of the sacred vessels.

Moreover, should the celebration acquire a theatrical aspect, it cannot properly be considered "worthy"; indeed, far from being a performance, a liturgical celebration has a primarily religious and spiritual dimension.

Lastly, this notion of worthiness implies the need to accompany celebrations with suitable movements for the liturgy. In other words, they should be made without haste but with a certain deliberation and elegance devoid of simulation.

Secondly, a liturgical celebration must be "attentive" and this demands of the celebrant a special effort so that, as far as possible, he may avoid distractions, especially voluntary ones. This adjective "attentive" permits insistence of the determination to focus one's spirit, which requires control of the senses if it is to avoid being swayed by the many objects that attract the gaze and distract the attention.

Music is naturally not in itself an obstacle to attention since it constitutes an integral part of the participation of the choir and the faithful, yet it is deplorable that certain liturgical celebrations do not foster the attention of the celebrant or the participants.

Indeed, the theatrical style of certain types of music gives excessive prominence to the prowess to the musicians or singers. This causes a harmful distraction in the faithful taking part in the liturgical celebration.

Thus, it is unseemly that the celebration of the Most Holy Eucharist be regarded in certain cases as an element in some way secondary to the performance of a famous piece of music that shows off the quality of the composer and the virtuosity of the performers. Unquestionably, this kind of practice is not conducive to strengthening the religious sense or recollection, whereas it is

appropriate to note that the use of Gregorian chant and high-quality polyphony that do justice to the liturgy are free from these particularly inauspicious consequences.

"Attention" requires silence; first and foremost, of course, "inner silence" or, if you will, a peaceful, tranquil heart. And this naturally implies external silence.

The whispering or comments of concelebrants to one another or to other ministers sitting near them reveals an undisciplined spirit and sets a bad example for the faithful.

On the other hand, a condition that prepares the ground for the attention that liturgical celebrants require is the effective preparation of the celebration so that it may take place in an orderly way without giving the impression that various elements have been left to improvisation.

Lastly, the celebration must be "devout." This implies an approach full of respect, love for God, a religious sense and attention to the "one thing" that "is necessary" (Luke 10:42).

In French, the adjective "devout" can be explained by the word "pious." "A devout person is one who is aware that his life has no meaning unless it is closely bound to God": this is one possible definition of the word "devout."

In other words, it is the attitude of all who desire to live a life totally consistent with their baptismal consecration, in accordance with the plan summed up concisely by Saint Paul: "If we live, we live to the Lord, and if we die, we die to the Lord; so then, whether we live or whether we die, we are the Lord's" (Romans 14:8). This means that a devout person is "totally dedicated to the Lord."

Those who take part in a liturgical action must not enter the sacred celebration having come straight to the community prayer from their profane, albeit respectable and honest, occupations. An interval marked by silence, recollection and prayer must elapse, even if it is only brief.

A striking example is set by monks who before entering the monastery church to celebrate the Divine Office—still called the Liturgy of the Hours—stand in the cloister in silence to focus their thoughts before concentrating on the recitation of the psalms.

The prayers the celebrant recites as he invests the liturgical vestments just before the beginning of the celebration serve the same purpose.

To conclude, we could say that the reflections expressed above ensue from the first of the dispositions required for an authentic participation in the liturgical celebration: it is faith that reveals the various rich meanings of the liturgical signs: faith, the only thing that enables the ordained minister to carry out his sacred role as Christ's instrument and the servant of his Body, the Holy Church.

The Grace of God

It is now indispensable to study another element essential for full participation in the liturgical celebration: the grace of God, or more precisely, the state of grace.

The goal of participation in liturgical actions is to obtain grace that is not yet possessed (as in the case of the baptism of children and access to the sacrament of Penance by those who are in a state of sin), as well as a growth of grace in those who are already justified. Grace is the concrete expression of salvation, the fruit of redemption and pledge of the glory that awaits us in the Kingdom of Heaven.

Being present at a liturgical celebration in a state of mortal sin and with no desire for conversion is not true participation, even if, during the celebration, the person concerned joins in the movements, hymns, acclamations or other gestures; for in this case, he lacks the fundamental orientation to God, and his glory that are the very soul of the liturgy.

This does not mean that those who do not possess the required inner disposition should be excluded from the celebration; for it is possible that their presence, even without all the conditions required for it to be defined true participation, may yet serve as an instrument of actual grace that will lead the person in question to conversion.

But people with a public reputation as sinners should be excluded from carrying out any service during the celebration, for this would be counterproductive and liable to cause scandal and confusion among the faithful. The assessment of various cases naturally calls for great pastoral prudence and a deeply sensitive approach.

It is appropriate, however, never to reduce the requirements provided for in the principles established by Church morals and law.

External Acts of Participation

In this day and age, in some rather unenlightened milieus which, moreover, have not been formed at the school of good theology, it is claimed that "participation" means no more that what is expressed by certain bodily attitudes. These, it is true, do express participation, but we should never forget that they are the external expressions of an internal participation.

In other words, we can say that these elements are the "material" and visible part of participation, whereas the "formal" element, in the strong or essential and invisible sense of the word, is constituted by the theological values—faith, hope, and charity—by the virtue of religion and by the state of grace; the latter alone puts the human creature in a state of consecration to the glory of God, on the basis of the coherence between the faith professed and the love of God and one's neighbor that is lived out in all life's decisions.

The Second Vatican Council identifies a certain number of elements intended to encourage active participation. Before citing them it is appropriate to make one very important observation: these elements do not alone or in themselves constitute liturgical participation; they do no more than express and foster it.

Indeed, it should always be remembered that the participation we can define as "substantial" derives from those elements presented, as we have said, as "formal."

This is the Conciliar text: "To promote active participation, the people should be encouraged to take part by means of acclamations, responses, psalms, antiphons, hymns, as well as by actions, gestures and bodily attitudes. And at the proper time a reverent silence should be observed. *When the liturgical books are being revised, the people's parts must be carefully indicated by the rubrics*" (SC, 30, 31).

It is obvious that the external elements of participation referred to in the conciliar text must not be ignored, since the human person, whose nature is both spiritual and corporeal, needs tangible expressions.

Furthermore, the external elements contribute to strengthening the internal dispositions.

Lastly, given that human beings are by nature inclined to live in society, they need tangible expressions that help them to live this experience of community life and to express worship as a social and not a solely private reality.

Thus, it is absolutely impossible to imagine a form of Catholic worship devoid of tangible elements. Above all, any attempt to eliminate from this worship expressions so connatural to human nature would deprive it of an essential part of what it is by nature.

Nor is it right to impose certain external attitudes too strictly, for fear of turning the liturgical celebration into a sequence of mechanical, hence, in a certain way, soulless gestures.

In this regard it must bed understood that different subjective situations can prompt someone to assume an attitude that does not rigorously conform to a specific moment, but this is no reason to speak of falling away from what has been described above as a "formal participation." Consequently, if a person does not rigorously respect this external action, it would be erroneous to presume that the person in question did not have the required dispositions for real and genuine participation.

Indeed, it can happen that some of those who celebrate the liturgy and carry out the external acts required by the rubrics with great attention to detail and rigorous discipline, are actually very farm from authentic inner participation.

The Ministries

The Constitution *Sacrosanctum Concilium*, 30, cited in the previous paragraph, concerns forms of participation that are "common" to the whole People of God.

However, there are also forms of participation that are special, in the sense that they are not obligatory for all the faithful nor, strictly speaking, do they entail the exercise of a "right"; on the other hand, they presuppose certain qualities and even an explicit reference on the part of those who are responsible for the smooth functioning of the liturgical celebration.

The Constitution on the Liturgy, *Sacrosanctum Concilium*, established this general principle: "In liturgical celebrations each person, minister or layman who has an office to perform, should carry

out all and only those parts which pertain to his office by the nature of the rite and the norms of the liturgy" (28).

Among the various liturgical ministries, it would be right first of all to mention all the functions which depend for fulfillment on those who through sacramental ordination are members of the clergy: Bishops, priests and deacons. It is the task of these ordained ministers to "structure" the Church, the visible Body of Christ, in which the sacred hierarchy is both the sign of salvation that comes from on high as a gratuitous gift and the instrument of saving action whose primary source is the Lord Jesus, the one Priest of the New Covenant who exercises his role as mediator through ordained ministers.

These ministers are so necessary that Saint Ignatius of Antioch declared that without a Bishop, priests or deacons, it was impossible to speak of a Church (cf. *Ad Trall*).

However, there are other non-ordained ministers who contribute to the dignity of the liturgical celebration.

We can name lectors who are responsible for reading the texts of Sacred Scripture but not the Gospel. The lector can be "instituted" (in this case he must necessarily be a man *[vir]*: CIC, 230.1), "blessed" or merely called upon for a specific celebration.

The office of reader is not a sign of honor or some kind of official recognition of a person's presumed merits. It is primarily and solely a service for the good of the People of God taking part in the celebrations.

It is important that lectors be respectable persons who have an irreprehensible ecclesial status, a good reputation and can also read well, that is, intelligibly and with a clear elocution that enable people to understand their articulation of the sentences of the sacred text.

Consequently, persons who may be very devout and respectable but are not gifted readers, that is, who are not good at making themselves understood by those taking part in the celebration, must not be called to the ministry of lector.

"Altar servers," also called "acolytes," may also be instituted (in this case, they must be adults and men [vir]: CIC, 230.1), "blessed" or merely called to carry out the service occasionally or on a more or less regular basis. They must be given appropriate training to fulfill their function with dignity, that is, without committing those errors that would necessarily jeopardize the quality and harmony of the celebration.

It is the duty of the diocesan Bishop, for a special reason and as an exception, to permit women or girls to exercise this ministry, but he should always be mindful of the Church's traditional preference for men and boys.[1]

Music is an integral part of liturgical celebrations, and this is why the Church down the centuries has recognized the role of the *schola cantorum* or choir. Its task is to interpret passages of liturgical music.

However, it is necessary to note in this regard that it would be abuse to allow the *schola cantorum* to encroach on the people's participation in the singing during the liturgical celebration. It would be even worse were the members of the *schola* to act in such a way as to attract attention to the detriment of the liturgical action, rather than abiding by their own role that consists in helping to build up the religious spirit of those taking part in liturgical celebrations.

The fact remains that the role of the *schola cantorum* is recognized by the Constitution on the Sacred Liturgy as a genuine liturgical function (cf. *Sacrosanctum Concilium*, 29).

The shortage of ordained ministers for the distribution of Holy Communion justifies the service of extraordinary ministers for the distribution of the Holy Eucharist. These ministers can be permanently instituted or called upon when necessary. Theirs is a temporary ministry and on no account a "promotion" of the laity.

The insufficient number of priest or deacons for the celebration of the sacrament of Baptism may lead the Bishop to authorize laypersons to be extraordinary ministers of this sacrament (cf. CIC, 230.3).[2] For the same reason, the Bishop may designate laypeople as qualified witnesses for the canonical celebration of marriage (CIC, 1112),[3] he may also authorize laypersons to lead Sunday celebrations in the absence of a priest (CIC, 1248.2, the Sacred Congregation for Divine Worship, Directory for Sunday Celebrations in the Absence of a Priest, *Christi Ecclesia*, 10 June 1988, Preliminaries, cf. *Notitiae* 263, 1988, 366–378)[4] or to preside at funerals (cf. *Ordo Exsequiarum, Praenotanda*, 19).[5]

Among the ministers who assist the ordained ministers in liturgical celebrations and especially in the celebration of the Most Holy Eucharist, is would be appropriate to recall the "master of ceremonies," who is responsible for seeing that the celebration takes place worthily and appropriately and that each of the ministers carries

out his role properly. This task is not strictly reserved to an ordained minister, priest or deacon, even if it is appropriate to choose a master of ceremonies from among them.

Lastly, the "commentator" should not be forgotten. It is he who, with brief and discreet instructions, helps the community to understand the various parts of the liturgical celebration.

It goes without saying that commentators must have a firm grasp of the meaning of the liturgical texts. This implies that they have been well instructed, for they may not provide interpretations of the rites celebrated at whim but must refer exclusively to the liturgical texts and actions approved by the Church.

The place in which commentators exercise their ministry is neither the pulpit nor the place for the proclamation of the Word, but somewhere else that is both suitable and discreet.

It is obvious that all who take part in a liturgical celebration and exercise such a "ministry" in it must take the trouble to prepare themselves, spiritually and liturgically. They must a acquire a knowledge, in the strict sense of the word of the norms that regulate a celebration and ensure that it takes place with dignity and is imbued with a religious spirit.

It would be right to insist once again on the fact that temporary ministries may be exercised only in the absence of ordained ministers or when ministers are in such short supply that it is impossible to see a celebration through within a reasonable period of time. It is indispensable therefore, to have clearly in mind the Inter-Dicasterial Instruction *Ecclesiae de Mysterio* on the collaboration of the lay faithful in the ministry of priests, published on 15 August 1997 (AAS 89, 1997, pp. 852–877; in a French translation: cf. *La Documentation Catholique*, 2171, 1997, 1009–1020).

Conclusion

The liturgy has an "ascendant" dimension, since it truly raises to the Majesty of God the praise that is due to him as Creator and Redeemer. This praise of the whole Church, Head and Body, is both personal and communal: it naturally involves every member of the faithful, but every member of the faithful also belongs to the Mystical Body of Christ.

And given that the Body of Christ, which is the Church has a structure established by her divine Founder, it is those who can act in *persona Christi*—since they have been admitted to share in apostolic succession by sacramental ordination—who preside at liturgical praise. Thus, this ascendant dimension culminates in the celebration of the Eucharistic Sacrifice.

However, it is true that the liturgy also has a "descendent" dimension, for it is through celebrations, and the celebration of the sacraments in particular, that salvation reaches human beings with sanctifying grace and all the gifts that go with it.

God, in his eternal plan of salvation for human beings, desired visible acts to convey invisible grace. Although these acts may be meant to make the person holy, they take form of liturgical celebrations in the community of believers, a concrete expression of Church.

Having come to the end of this reflection, it seems to me particularly timely to return to the first text of the Constitution on the Second Vatican Council on the Holy Liturgy. This is the text: "It is the liturgy through which, especially in the divine sacrifice of the Eucharist, 'the work of our redemption is accomplished' and it is through the liturgy, especially, that the faithful are enabled to express in their lives and manifest to others the mystery of Christ and the real nature of the true Church. The Church is essentially both human and divine, visible but endowed with invisible realities, zealous in action and dedicated to contemplation, present in the world but as a pilgrim, so constituted that in her the human is directed toward and subordinated to the divine, the visible to the invisible, action to contemplation, and this present world to that city yet to come, the object of our quest" (*Sacrosanctum Concilium*, 2).

The subject of participation in liturgical celebrations truly makes tangible to us the mystery of salvation, the wonderful economy with which the merciful Father, through his Incarnate Word, reveals his plan to us and bring it about through the power of the Holy Spirit who makes all things new.

---

1. The circular Letter of 15 March 1994 of the Congregation for Divine Worship and the Discipline of the Sacraments to the Presidents of the Bishops' Conferences (*Notitiae* 39, 1994, 333–335), on the application of the

Response of The Pontifical Council for the Interpretation of Legislative Texts with regard to the authentic interpretation of canon 203.2 (according to this canon, do the liturgical functions that laypersons can fulfill include altar service? *Affirmative et iuxta instructiones a Sede Apostolica dandas*. Cf. AAS 86, 1994, 541), established that it is the task of each Bishop in his own Diocese, after hearing the opinion of the Bishops' Conference, to issue a prudent judgment on the appropriate action for the harmonious development of liturgical life in his own Diocese.

Moreover, the obligation to continue to prefer boys for altar service, which has permitted an encouraging development in priestly vocations, will always exist. In a Letter of 27 July 2001 (*Notitiae* 421–422, 2001, 397–399), the Congregation for Divine Worship and the Discipline of the Sacraments explains on the one hand that the freedom of the diocesan Bishop cannot be conditioned by possible decisions of neighboring Bishops who favor altar service carried out by women, and on the other hand, that the possible authorization of the Bishop must always leave priest of his Diocese free to have recourse to a group of altar servers consisting only of boys, give the obligation contained in the Letter of 1994, cited above, concerning the growth of priestly vocations.

2. The Inter-Dicasterial Instruction *Ecclesiae de Mysterio* of 15 August 1997 (Practical Provisions, art. 11) explains that care should be taken to avoid too extensive an interpretation of this provision and to ensure that such a faculty is not conceded in a habitual form.

For example, the absence or the impediment of a sacred minister which renders licit the deputation of the lay faithful to act as an extraordinary minister of Baptism, cannot be defined in terms of the ordinary minister's excessive workload, his non-residence in the territory of the parish or his nonavailability on the day on which the family have planned the Baptism. Such reasons are insufficient.

3. Canon 1112 requires the prior favorable opinion of the Bishops' Conference and the permission of the Holy See. In France this possibility of delegating faculties to laypersons does not exist.

4. The Inter-Dicasterial Instruction *Ecclesiae de Mysterio* of 15 August 1997 (Practical Provisions, art. 7) explains that the non-ordained member of the faithful who leads this kind of celebration must have a special mandate from the Bishop, who will take care to provide the appropriate instructions regarding the term of applicability, the place and conditions in which it is operative, as well as to indicate the priest responsible.

Furthermore, these celebrations are temporary solutions and the text used at them must be approved by the competent ecclesiastical authority. The practices of inserting into such celebrations elements proper to the Holy Mass and the use of the Eucharistic Prayers even in narrative form are forbidden.

It should be emphasized for the benefit of those participating that such celebrations cannot substitute for the Eucharistic Sacrifice and that the obligation to attend Mass on Sunday and holy days of obligation is satisfied only at attendance at Holy Mass, even at the cost of taking part in a Sunday celebration in the absence of a priest, when participation in the Holy Sacrifice is not possible. In the cases where distance or physical conditions are not an obstacle, every effort should be made to encourage and assist the faithful to fulfill this precept (AAS 89, 1997, 869–870).

5. The Inter-Dicasterial Instruction *Ecclesiae de Mysterio* of 15 August 1997 (Practical Provisions, art. 12) recalls that this possibility only exists in the case of a true absence of sacred ministers. Moreover, because of the present circumstances of growing dechristianization and of abandonment of religious practice, death and the time of funerals can become one of the most opportune pastoral moments in which the ordained minister can meet with the non-practicing members of the faithful.

It is thus desirable that priests and deacons, even at some sacrifice to themselves *(cum magna deditione),* should preside personally at funeral rites (AAS 89, 1997,874).

Sacrosanctum Concilium Anniversary Address: The Foundations of Liturgical Reform

Francis Cardinal George, OMI

INTRODUCTION

The fortieth anniversary of the promulgation of *Sacrosanctum Concilium* has prompted a flurry of meetings, discussions and symposia. It remains a document of keen interest to us because of the central and crucial role of the liturgy in the life of the Church. The subject is broad and vast, however, and difficult to summarize in a forty-minute presentation.

Other bishops, extremely competent in the field of liturgy, have already treated this topic: I am thinking in particular of Bishop Tena Garriga, auxiliary of Barcelona, who gave a masterful address on *Sacrosanctum Concilium* in this very aula in the year 2000, in the context of the Jubilee Year celebrations.[1] Quite recently, Cardinal Sodano, in a letter to the participants of the Italian National Liturgy Week (August 25–29, 2003) also gave an overview of *Sacrosanctum Concilium*, listing a number of areas of research that remain to be explored, namely, the relationship between:
1. creativity and fidelity;
2. spiritual worship and life;
3. catechesis and the celebration of the Mystery;
4. presiding at the liturgy and the role of the congregation;
5. seminary formation and the continuing formation of priests.[2]

There remains yet another aspect of the liturgical reform that requires further study, the anthropological aspect. For this presentation, I think it might be fruitful to sketch out some of the main questions

that present themselves in the philosophical and anthropological areas of the liturgical reform. It is my hope that the questions thus formulated might spark investigations that are more scholarly and in-depth in an area that requires interdisciplinary collaboration. This approach also brings to the fore many pastoral considerations that have arisen from liturgical change.

My own belief is that liturgical renewal after the Council was treated as a program or movement for change, without enough thought being given to what happens in any community when its symbol system is disrupted. The liturgical calendar, for example is the place where time and eternity meet, when our experience or duration transcends itself through contact with the Creator of time and history. To change the liturgical calendar means to change our way of relating to God. Since time also conditions thinking for embodied spirits, whose reasoning entails a return to a phantasm, the doctrines of the Church's faith, the thinking of the Church, will also be considered differently when liturgical time is changed. Pastorally, every bishop has been asked: "Since we no longer recognize certain saints on the Church's calendar, why can't the Church correct her teaching on sexual morality, on women's ordination and on other difficult doctrines?" A change in space, in architecture and in the placement of altars and other liturgical furnishings, has similar effect, as has a change in language, which carries and conditions our thinking and evaluating. A change in liturgy changes the context of the Church's life. Recently, introducing the changes mandated by the new *General Instruction of the Roman Missal* (third typical edition), I remarked that the changes were "minor." A laywoman of the Archdiocese of Chicago corrected me: "Cardinal, there are no minor changes in liturgy." She is correct.

I would like to raise the question here in order to clarify the presuppositions of liturgical change and so to advance the liturgical renewal with self-conscious attention to the pastoral context as well as to liturgical theory. The questions are raised not to bring the renewal itself into question but to strengthen its call to the Church and its effects in the Church. This presentation will be guided by two questions: 1) Who is the subject of the liturgy? and 2) How does that subject participate in the liturgy? I will look at the subject from three more or less different angles: theological, philosophical and anthropological, in each case asking what has yet to be explored.

I. The Subject of the Liturgy Considered from a Theological Point of View

A. Who Is the Subject of the Liturgy?

Sacrosanctum Concilium, 7, continuing in the tradition of *Mediator Dei*, defines the liturgy as the exercise of the priestly office of Jesus Christ. Hence, it is the whole Christ, Head and members who are the subject of the liturgy. The text goes on to say that the earthly liturgy is a participation in the heavenly one (SC, 8); this affirmation expands the subject of the liturgy to include the heavenly host of angels and all the saints. Since the first section of *Sacrosanctum Concilium* (the nature of the liturgy and its significance in the life of the Church) is deliberately brief, these very important points are not further developed. Aspects of the theology of the liturgy were taken up again in *Lumen gentium* and *Dei verbum*, and the area of liturgical theology has been the subject of serious reflection in the last forty years. The greatest magisterial development of this issue, however, can be found in the *Catechism of the Catholic Church*. This surely fits under the category of development of doctrine, because the Catechism's treatment of the subject of the liturgy takes a significant step forward that is at once disarmingly simple and wonderfully profound. The liturgy is *Opus Trinitatis*, the work of the Holy Trinity (CCC, 1077, title).[3] While *Sacrosanctum Concilium* focuses on the Christological aspect of the liturgy, the new Catechism meditates at length on the role of the Father and of the Holy Spirit as well. In fact, it is the relatively lengthy section on the Holy Spirit (CCC, 1091–1109) which makes a remarkable contribution to a new Trinitarian understanding of the liturgy. While the Catechism cites SC, 8, verbatim on the heavenly liturgy (CCC, 1090), it also goes a step further by devoting nine paragraphs (CCC, 1136–1144) to the question "Who celebrates the liturgy?" First of all there are the celebrants of the heavenly liturgy: the Father, Son and Holy Spirit: the persons of the Trinity are the primary actors in the liturgy. Then come the heavenly powers, all creation, biblical saints, the martyrs, the all-holy Mother of God and the great multitude of the elect. The earthly liturgy exists not by itself, but in relation to the heavenly liturgy. The celebrants of the sacramental liturgy include the entire Body of Christ extending through time and space, then the local

celebrating assembly, ordered hierarchically in such a way that each person has his proper role.

Clarity about the theological subject of the liturgy is crucial. In the post-conciliar period, a limited understanding of the "People of God" has often led to a limited, horizontal concept of the subject of the liturgy. Hence it is extremely important that this wonderfully complete vision of the liturgy, earthly united to heavenly, becomes better known and then internalized and lived.

B. Theologically, How Does the Earthly Liturgy Participate in the Heavenly Liturgy?

The question of participation is perhaps the overriding preoccupation of *Sacrosanctum Concilium*. The text refers over and over again to a participation which is *sciens, actuosa, fructuosa, conscia, plena, pia, facilus, interna, externa*, and so on. But how does that participation take place?[4] Here the conciliar document is rather reticent. Here also the last forty years have given us examples of participation which range from the sublime to the ridiculous. Once again, it is the Catechism which makes significant strides in this area. The church participates in the liturgy by *synergy*. This idea comes from the fruitful synthesis of Father Jean Corbon, whose insights in his book *Wellspring of Worship*[5] will appear later in the Catechism. Participation is the common work or synergy between divine initiative and human response. The agent who makes participation possible is the Holy Spirit. "When the Spirit encounters in us the response of faith which he has aroused in us, he brings about genuine cooperation. Through it, the liturgy becomes the common work of the Holy Spirit and the Church" (CCC, 1091). The Holy Spirit prepares the faithful for the reception of Christ (CCC, 1093–1098), recalls the mystery of Christ (CCC, 1099–1103), makes present the mystery of Christ (CCC, 1104–1107) and brings about that communion which is an anticipation of the fullness of communion with the Holy Trinity (CCC, 1107–1109). In fact, the most intimate cooperation, or synergy, of the Holy Spirit and the Church is achieved in the liturgy (CCC, 1108). Without insistent reference to the Holy Spirit, the Holy Eucharist might easily come to be imagined as a recreation of the Last Supper, a sort of memorial tableau, rather

than a re-presentation in unbloody, symbolic forms of the sacrifice of Calvary.

In the magisterium of the Church—in particular in *Sacrosanctum Concilium* and the *Catechism of the Catholic Church*—the liturgical subject is clearly delineated from a theological point of view, and the question of participation at its most profound theological level is wonderfully illustrated. Much remains to be done to communicate this teaching more effectively and to internalize it, but the teaching itself is clear.

What is less clear is its philosophical underpinnings. Under this rubric we will consider the nature of the human person who celebrates the liturgy.

II. The Subject of the Liturgy Considered from a Philosophical Point of View

A. Who Is the Personal Subject of the Liturgy?

The human person as the subject of the liturgy can be considered philosophically from three points of view. First, SC refers to the individual subject of the liturgy simply as *homo*. It is clear that the text is referring to man as such, in a generic sense. The fields of study here are the philosophy of man and epistemology. The questions are: what is the nature of the human person and how does he know? These are areas which the Council did not have explicitly on its agenda. Secondly, SC also uses the term *fidelis*, or man as a Christian believer. The discipline here is theological anthropology; the conciliar constitution, *Gaudium, et spes*, took some first steps but their use of terms such as "modern man" and "the modern world" lack a clearly defined framework for their interpretation, a lack that has had unfortunate effect for the development of liturgical forms in the postmodern mass culture. (See Tracy Rowland, London: Routledge, 2003, *Culture and the Thomist Tradition after Vatican II*, pp. 18–21, 168). In this situation the question becomes more specific: how does the believer know divine realities? Thirdly, anthropologists have coined the phrase *homo liturgicus*, since we are dealing with man as he lives and acts in a liturgical context. This is a new category of philosophical investigation, unknown to the Council Fathers, where the waters are not yet

completely charted. The philosophical question now is: how does this man, who believes, know divine realities as communicated in the liturgy?[6]

1. Pauline Anthropology

Saint Paul's letters reveal a sophisticated anthropology, although difficult to put into a system. He speaks of the various constitutive elements of the human person as soma (body), *sarx* (flesh), *psyche* (soul), *pneuma* (spirit), *nous* (mind), and *kardia* (heart). How does the Christian, considered under those polyvalent aspects, know the world around him? How does he grasp the things of God?

2. Patristic Anthropology

In patristic ascetical theology, one frequently finds a description of the soul as tri-partite: the *logikon* or rational part, the *thumikon* or irascible part, and the *epithumikon* or concupiscible part. How does man, understood in this way, respond to the exterior world? How does he apprehend reality, if not by means of reason, emotion and sense perception? Here is a classic synthesis that will remain a constant point of reference throughout the centuries.

3. Thomistic Anthropology

When Saint Thomas asks the question of the specific powers of the soul (I, q.78, a.1), he takes the triple distinction of the tradition (the soul described as rational, sensitive and vegetative) and develops it with extraordinary subtlety and insight. At the risk of grossly oversimplifying, we can say that the vegetative part includes nutritive, augmentative and generative elements; the sensitive part includes the five exterior senses as well as five interior senses (common sense, fantasy, imagination, and the estimative and memorative senses); and the intellectual part includes such aspects as memory, understanding, and will.

It would be worthwhile for his tightly ordered reasoning to be unpacked and explained for the sake of the non-specialist, for here is a very sophisticated analysis of how man knows, how he perceives both interior realities and the exterior world in which he lives. This kind

of philosophical reasoning could be very helpful in trying to understand how *homo liturgicus* perceives natural and supernatural realities.[7]

4. Enlightenment Anthropology

In terms of epistemology, the Enlightenment rationalist position affirms that reason alone is the source of knowledge and the ultimate test of truth. Revelation as a specific source of knowledge is denied. Human powers, other than reason, such as sense perception, imagination and intuition are downplayed. While positive elements of rationalist thought can be seen in a rejection of prejudice, ignorance and superstition, the logical consequences of the rationalist position sooner or later lead to the profound secularization experienced in the western world today.

A moderate Enlightenment position would grant worship some role in human life, since religion has its purpose, according to this point of view, the inculcation of moral virtue. Thus religious instruction, not the worship of God, was seen as the central point of church services. The liturgy thus risks being reduced to a pedagogical aid.

There are studies today in German[8] and English[9] which argue that the roots of the twentieth-century liturgical movement, and hence of the post-conciliar liturgical reforms as well, lie in the Enlightenment, with all the attendant positive and negative consequences. These studies merit serious attention.

For our purposes, the question here is how man, understood in this rationalistic sense, interacts with the world and understands supernatural realities.

5. Romantic Anthropology

It is not surprising that the extraordinary force of Enlightenment thought would provoke an equal and opposite reaction. The Romantic response was to emphasize all those things that rationalism denied: sense experience, imagination, intuition, sentiment. This experiential emphasis became the hallmark of a new movement in art and literature. In the life of the Church, the positive aspects of this movement were a rediscovery of the medieval period, a new God-centeredness, and a high theology of the Church as the Mystical Body of Christ. Romanticism is not without its negative consequences, however, such

as piety without dogma, subjectivism, an exaggerated emphasis on feeling, and a kind of "cosmic nature." How does man know? The romantic answer might be: he feels.

6. *Contemporary Period*

The contemporary period seems to be heir to this dichotomy between Enlightenment and Romantic movements. The dominant view is still a rationalist one, but the vigor of the romantic reaction is striking. It is ironic that John Paul II, in his encyclical *Fides et Ratio*, would have to defend reason itself in the face of a massive movement of popular culture toward New Age spiritualism. In the area of the liturgy, this same dichotomy finds expression in a multitude of ways. The reality is a complex one, different in different places, but liturgical polarization between a rationalist and a romantic position is common, and few people have the tools necessary to move beyond the present impasse.[10]

A curious concept which seems to be in the air we breathe, an idea born of evolutionary theories and the experience of scientific progress in the nineteenth and twentieth centuries, is that man is always progressing, getting better and better. The myth of human progress replaces salvation history. It is said that modern man is more advanced than in ages past, and therefore cannot be understood according to categories of earlier times. While it is true that technological changes have revolutionized the way we live, how true is it that the *nature* of man has changed? *Sacrosanctum Concilium* can give the impression of ambiguity in this regard, referring frequently to the need to adapt liturgical structures and forms to the needs of our time (SC, 1), to contemporary needs and circumstances (SC, 4). It is also necessary to explore the question of how man needs to adapt to the demands of modern man.

B. How Does the Personal Subject Participate in the Liturgy?

Given the polyvalent reality which is man, and the difficulties of formulating how the individual subject knows, it is with some caution that we approach the topic philosophically of how the human person participates in the liturgy. *Scarosanctum Concilium* appears to set up a dual approach. First of all, the Christian people must understand, then they will be able to participate.

Words most frequently used for understanding are *intellegere* and *percipere*. To foster this understanding, there is a heavy emphasis on catechesis and instruction (cf. SC, 35/3). Our understanding of the liturgy should be readily accessible or easy *(facile)* (cf. SC, 21, 50, 59, 79, etc.). If we apply the tri-partite anthropology discussed earlier, it seems that the conciliar text is emphasizing a rational understanding of *ritus et preces*. The aspect of intuition and imagination is not discussed, nor the apprehension of reality by sense experience. In all fairness it should be said that *Sacrosanctum Concilium* does not pretend to give an exhaustive treatment of liturgical epistemology, nor could the Council Fathers have possibly imagined the pastoral situations that would arise in subsequent years which would require a more nuanced and sophisticated treatment of this topic.

By understanding the liturgy more easily, so the reasoning goes, the Christian believer is better able to participate in it. While the conciliar text mentions interior as well as exterior participation (SC, 19), and states that sacred silence is also a form of participation (SC, 30), the emphasis is on verbal response and physical gesture (SC, 30), and in fact, the post-conciliar experience is one of an extremely verbal liturgy with much activity going on. The more profound understanding of participation, not in the external, visible sense, but in the sacramental, internal and visible dimension[11] is not elaborated by *Sacrosanctum Concilium*. What is needed, therefore, is a more unified vision of man and a more profound understanding of liturgical participation. The human person understands the liturgy by means of reason, without a doubt. The best and brightest intellect has ample material for reflection in the rich complex truths which the liturgy expresses. At the same time, the human experiences the liturgy through emotion and feeling, through an aesthetic appreciation of beauty, through the intuitive making of connections, through associations which take place on the subliminal level. This kind of human knowing should not be undervalued. And finally, man experiences the liturgy though the five senses, which is the human foundation of the sacramental system. This sensory experience has the capacity to open up spiritual realities, as the famous text of Tertullian says:

> The body is washed so that the soul may be freed from its stains; the body is anointed, so that the soul too may be consecrated; the body is signed, so that the soul too may be strengthened.[12]

In addition to a renewed philosophical investigation of the nature of man and how he participates in the liturgy, a third field of study which is extremely important is that of cultural anthropology.

III. The Subject of the Liturgy from the Point of View of Cultural Anthropology

A. Who Is the Subject of the Liturgy?

The cultural anthropologist examines not only the individual subject, but also the communal subject of the liturgy, that is, the ritual assembly. In the liturgy the celebrating community is usually a heterogeneous gathering of people: old and young, rich and poor, "male and female, slave and free, Jew and Gentile" (as Saint Paul would say), from every level of society, gathered together not because of some common human element, but because God who transcends every human category, calls them together. For such an unlikely combination of people to act together as one, something extraordinary must take place. From the theological point of view, what happens is the synergy between the Holy Spirit and the Church which we spoke about earlier. From an anthropological and sociological point of view, what happens is a specific kind of ritual behavior.

B. How Does That Subject Participate in the Liturgy?

The ritual assembly participates in the liturgy according to a complex set of rules and roles. The activity is ceremonious, formal, repetitive. What happens this Sunday is the same as what happened last Sunday, for authentic ritual functions according to disciplined patterns of habit and continuity. This kind of participation avoids spontaneity and on-the-spot adaptation in favor of the predictable and the familiar. The vehicle of expression includes words, but relies more heavenly on symbols and symbolic actions. The more profound symbols have many levels of meaning, are "opaque" in that sense, are not susceptible to superficial and easy understanding. Symbols are always self-involving, objective in a way that incorporates the subjective. The qualities of beauty and holiness are communicated by signs which are the product of the highest cultural achievement. Immersion

in the ritual action takes the participants out of themselves and transforms them.

On the other hand, numerous and rapid changes in ritual forms can produce estrangement and *anomie,* an experience reported by many of the faithful in the post-conciliar years.

In recent decades, ritual activity has been the object of study by the relatively new discipline of social anthropology. This discipline began to come onto its own a decade or so after the promulgation of *Sacrosanctum Concilium,* and thus the valuable insights of social anthropology simply were not available at the time of the drafting of the conciliar text and the formulation of the liturgical reforms, although we can see perhaps an oblique reference in the assertion that liturgical change must respect the general laws of the structure and *mens* of the liturgy (SC, 23). Aidan Nichols observes: "The postconciliar *Consilium ad exsequendam Constitutionem de Sacra Liturgia* was wound up in 1975 through absorption into the Congregation for Divine Worship, that year coinciding more or less with a real turning point in the anthropology of religion as new schools of thought began to emphasize meaning, not explanation, the non-rational as well as the rational, and ritual's transformative power: all of which led to a new respect for the formal, ceremonious ordering of rite . . . ."[13] From the point of view of social anthropology, it is not self-evident that simplicity in ritual form is more effective than complexity. It is not clear that a sign which is immediately intelligible will be more effective than a multi-faceted symbol which reveals its meaning only over time. In short, simplifying ritual action will not necessarily bring about the greater understanding and more active participation desired by the Council.[14]

Further work in the area of social anthropology, then could provide insight into the many open questions concerning liturgical participation.

Conclusion

We must hope that forty years of experience since the promulgation of *Sacrosanctum Concilium* will lead us from a kind of naive innocence to a wisdom shaped by pastoral shrewdness. The difference between the two, of course, is the knowledge of good and evil. Experience teaches

us that in this area, which is so vital to the Church's life, an interdisciplinary approach can bear much fruit. While much work has been done in the area of liturgical theology, not enough has been done in the fields of philosophy, epistemology and cultural anthropology. In addition to wise pastoral action in liturgical matters, what is also necessary is renewed theoretical study, serious and in-depth, of these open questions which I have tried to delineate. This has to part of a critical re-reading of the Constitutions and other documents of Vatican II in light of such development in understanding and of the experience of the past 40 years.

---

1. P. Tena Garriga, *La sacra liturgia fonte e culmine della vita ecclesiale*, in: *Il Concilio Vaticano II: Recezionne e attualità alla luce del Giubileo*, San Paolo, Roma 2000, pp. 46–65.

2. A. Sodano, "For the Celebration of Italian National Liturgy Week," in: *L'Osservatore Romano*, English edition 39 (24 September 2003), p. 4.

3. Father Jeremy Driscoll throws light on this with his comment that the Christian taking part in the liturgy is "a person who can participate in the community of Divine Persons," indeed who is "created for this in the image of the Divine Persons" (J. Driscoll, "Liturgy and Fundamental Theology," in *Ecclesia Orans*, 11 [1994/1], 79).

4. Contrary to popular, and sometimes academic, misconceptions, active participation in the liturgy is not first of all saying, reading or taking part in rites. It is primarily, essentially and indispensably the devotion of mind, heart and will elicited and brought into vital contact with Christ through the rites. The Latin word *devotio* signifies consecration to God (O. Casel, *The Mystery of Christian Worship*, New York: Herder and Herder, 1999, p. 36). For the liturgy to be fruitful in a person's life there has to be a subjective dimension; those taking part must cooperate with and accept inwardly the act of Jesus the Priest by their devotion (cf. Pope Pius XII, *Mediator Dei*, 28, 29; CCC, 2563).

5. J. Corbon, *The Wellspring of Worship*, Mahwah, New Jersey: Paulist Press, 1988.

6. The implications of this question, though not as yet fully taken account of by many liturgists, have begun to be spelled out by anthropologists such as Victor Turner who writes, "If ritual is not to be merely a reflection of secular social life, if its function is partly to protect and partly to express truths which make men free from the exigencies of their status-incumbencies, free to contemplate and pray as well as to speculate and invent, then its repertoire

of liturgical actions should not be limited to a direct reflection of the contemporary scene" (V. Turner, "Passages, Margins, and Poverty: Symbols of Communitas," in *Worship,* 46 [1972], p. 391). Traditional liturgy, precisely because of its archaic quality, has power to modify and even reverse the assumptions made in secular living; the archaic is not the obsolete.

7. See J. Driscoll, "Deepening the Theological Dimensions of Liturgical Studies", in *Communio,* 23, Fall 1996, pp. 513–514. This article shows how pre-rational instincts and rhythms make possible an expression of God's Word in human words.

8. W. Trapp, *Vorgeschichte and Ursprung der liturgischen Bewegung: vorwiegend im Hinsicht auf das deutsche Sprachgebiet,* Regensburg, 1940.

9. A. Nichols, *Looking at the Liturgy: A Critical View of Its Contemporary Form,* San Francisco: Ignatius Press, 1996.

10. A noteworthy exception to this is the paper delivered by Stratford Caldecott at the Fontgombault Liturgical Conference in July 2001, titled *Liturgy and Trinity: Towards an Anthropology of the Liturgy* in *Looking Again at the Question of the Liturgy with Cardinal Ratzinger,* Alguin Reed, ed., Farnborough: St. Augustine's Press, 2003, pp. 36–48.

11. Cf. the masterful analysis of Saint Cyril of Jerusalem's theology of sacramental participation by E. Mazza, *Mystagogy: A Theology of Liturgy in the Patristic Age,* Collegeville, Minnesota: The Liturgical Press, 1989, pp. 150–164.

12. Tertulllian, *De Carnis Resurrectione,* 8.

13. A. Nichols, *Looking at the Liturgy,* p. 57.

14. Further and well-documented evidence for this is given by Dr. Tracey Rowland (*Culture and the Thomistic Tradition,* pp. 27–29, 168, 69 on p. 175) where she outlines the dilemma created when, in the wake of Vatican II, and because of some assumptions of the architects of *Sacrosanctum Concilium,* the forms of the liturgy come to be dominated by the postmodern mass culture.

Appendix

Appendix

Constitution on the Sacred Liturgy
Sacrosanctum Concilium

Second Vatican Council

4 December 1963

Outline

Introduction 1–4

Chapter I: General Principles for the Reform and Promotion of the Sacred Liturgy 5–46
    I. Nature of the Liturgy and its Importance in the Church's Life 5–13
    II. Promotion of Liturgical Instruction and Active Participation 14–20
    III. The Reform of the Sacred Liturgy 21–40
        A. General Norms 22–25
        B. Norms Drawn from the Hierarchic and Communal Nature of the Liturgy 26–32
        C. Norms Based on the Teaching and Pastoral Character of the Liturgy 33–36
        D. Norms for Adapting the Liturgy to the Culture and Traditions of Peoples 37–40
    IV. Promotion of Liturgical Life in Diocese and Parish 41–42
    V. Promotion of Pastoral-Liturgical Action 43–46

Chapter II: The Most Sacred Mystery of the Eucharist 47–58
Chapter III: The Other Sacraments and the Sacramentals 59–82
Chapter IV: Divine Office 83–101
Chapter V: The Liturgical Year 102–111
Chapter VI: Sacred Music 112–121
Chapter VII: Sacred Art and Sacred Furnishings 122–130
Appendix: Declaration of the Second Vatican Ecumenical Council on Revision of the Calendar 131

Constitution on the Sacred Liturgy

1. This Sacred Council has several aims in view: it desires to impart an ever increasing vigor to the Christian life of the faithful; to adapt more suitably to the needs of our own times those institutions that are subject to change; to foster whatever can promote union among all who believe in Christ; to strengthen whatever can help to call the whole of humanity into the household of the Church. The Council therefore sees particularly cogent reasons for undertaking the reform and promotion of the liturgy.

2. For the liturgy, "making the work of our redemption a present actuality,"[1] most of all in the divine sacrifice of the eucharist, is the outstanding means whereby the faithful may express in their lives and manifest to others the mystery of Christ and the real nature of the true Church. It is of the essence of the Church to be both human and divine, visible yet endowed with invisible resources, eager to act yet intent on contemplation, present in this world yet not at home in it; and the Church is all these things in such wise that in it the human is directed and subordinated to the divine, the visible likewise to the invisible, action to contemplation, and this present world to that city yet to come which we seek.[2] While the liturgy daily builds up those who are within into a holy temple of the Lord, into a dwelling place for God in the Spirit,[3] to the mature measure of the fullness of Christ,[4] at the same time it marvelously strengthens their power to preach Christ and thus shows forth the Church to those who are outside as a sign lifted up among the nations,[5] under which the scattered children of God may be gathered together,[6] until there is one sheepfold and one shepherd.[7]

3. Wherefore the Council judges that the following principles concerning the promotion and reform of the liturgy should be called to mind and practical norms established.

Among these principles and norms there are some that can and should be applied both to the Roman Rite and also to all the other rites. The practical norms that follow, however, should be taken as applying only to the Roman Rite, except for those that, in the very nature of things, affect other rites as well.

4. Lastly, in faithful obedience to tradition, the Council declares that the Church holds all lawfully acknowledged rites to be of equal right and dignity and wishes to preserve them in the future and to foster them in every way. The Council also desires that, where necessary, the rites be revised carefully in the light of sound tradition and that they be given new vigor to meet the circumstances and needs of modern times.

Chapter I
General Principles for the Reform and Promotion of the Sacred Liturgy

I. Nature of the Liturgy and Its Importance in the Church's Life

5. God who "wills that all be saved and come to the knowledge of the truth" (1 Tm. 2:4), "who in many and various ways spoke in times past to the fathers by the prophets" (Heb. 1:1), when the fullness of time had come sent his Son, the Word made flesh, anointed by the Holy Spirit, to preach the Gospel to the poor, to heal the contrite of heart;[1] he is "the physician, being both flesh and of the Spirit,"[2] the mediator between God and us.[3] For his humanity, united with the person of the Word, was the instrument of our salvation. Therefore in Christ "the perfect achievement of our reconciliation came forth and the fullness of divine worship was given to us.[4]

The wonderful works of God among the people of the Old Testament were a prelude to the work of Christ the Lord. He achieved his task of redeeming humanity and giving perfect glory to God, principally by the paschal mystery of his blessed passion, resurrection from the dead, and glorious ascension, whereby "dying, he destroyed our death and, rising, he restored our life."[5] For it was from the side of Christ as he slept the sleep of death upon the cross that there came forth the sublime sacrament of the whole Church.[6]

6. As Christ was sent by the Father, he himself also sent the apostles, filled with the Holy Spirit. Their mission was, first, by preaching the Gospel to every creature,[7] to proclaim that by his death and resurrection Christ has freed us from Satan's grip[8] and brought us into the Father's kingdom. But the work they preached they were also to bring into effect through the sacrifice and the sacraments, the center of the whole liturgical life. Thus by baptism all are plunged into the paschal mystery of Christ: they die with him, are buried with him, and rise with him;[9] they receive the spirit of adoption as children "in which we cry: Abba, Father" (Rom. 8:15), and thus become true adorers whom the Father seeks.[10] In like manner, as often as they eat the supper of the Lord they proclaim the death of the Lord until he comes.[11] For that reason, on the very day of Pentecost when the Church appeared before the world, "those who received the word" of Peter "were baptized." And "they continued steadfastly in the teaching of the apostles and in the communion of the breaking of bread and in prayers . . . praising God and being in favor with all the people" (Acts 2:41–47). From that time onward the Church has never failed to come together to celebrate the paschal mystery: reading those things "which were in all the Scriptures concerning him" (Lk. 24:27); celebrating the eucharist, in which "the victory and triumph of his death are again made present";[12] and at the same time giving thanks "to God for his

inexpressible gift" (2 Cor. 9:15) in Christ Jesus, "in praise of his glory" (Eph. 1:12), through the power of the Holy Spirit.

7. To accomplish so great a work, Christ is always present in his Church, especially in its liturgical celebrations. He is present in the sacrifice of the Mass, not only in the person of his minister, "the same now offering, through the ministry of priests, who formerly offered himself on the cross,"[13] but especially under the eucharistic elements. By his power he is present in the sacraments, so that when a man baptizes it is really Christ himself who baptizes.[14] He is present in his word, since it is he himself who speaks when the holy Scriptures are read in the Church. He is present, lastly, when the Church prays and sings, for he promised: "Where two or three are gathered together in my name, there am I in the midst of them" (Mt. 18:20).

Christ always truly associates the Church with himself in this great work wherein God is perfectly glorified and the recipients made holy. The Church is the Lord's beloved Bride who calls to him and through him offers worship to the eternal Father.

Rightly, then, the liturgy is considered as an exercise of the priestly office of Jesus Christ. In the liturgy, by means of signs perceptible to the senses, human sanctification is signified and brought about in ways proper to each of these signs; in the liturgy the whole public worship is performed by the Mystical Body of Jesus Christ, that is, by the Head and his members.

From this it follows that every liturgical celebration, because it is an action of Christ the Priest and of his Body which is the Church, is a sacred action surpassing all others; no other action of the Church can equal its effectiveness by the same title and to the same degree.

8. In the earthly liturgy we take part in a foretaste of that heavenly liturgy celebrated in the holy city of Jerusalem toward which we journey as pilgrims, where Christ is sitting at the right hand of God, a minister of the holies and of the true tabernacle;[15] we sing a hymn to the Lord's glory with the whole company of heaven; venerating the memory of the saints, we hope for some part and fellowship with them; we eagerly await the Savior, our Lord Jesus Christ, until he, our life, shall appear and we too will appear with him in glory.[16]

9. The liturgy does not exhaust the entire activity of the Church. Before people can come to the liturgy they must be called to faith and to conversion: "How then are they to call upon him in whom they have not yet believed? But how are they to believe him whom they have not heard? And how are they to hear if no one preaches? And how are men to preach unless they be sent?" (Rom. 10:14–15).

Therefore the Church announces the good tidings of salvation to those who do not believe, so that all may know the true God and Jesus Christ whom he has sent and may be converted from their ways, doing penance.[17] To believers, also, the Church must ever preach faith and penance, prepare them for the sacraments, teach them to observe all that Christ has commanded,[18]

and invite them to all the works of charity, worship, and the apostolate. For all these works make it clear that Christ's faithful, though not of this world, are to be the light of the world and to glorify the Father in the eyes of all.

10. Still, the liturgy is the summit toward which the activity of the Church is directed; at the same time it is the fount from which all the Church's power flows. For the aim and object of apostolic works is that all who are made children of God by faith and baptism should come together to praise God in the midst of his Church, to take part in the sacrifice, and to eat the Lord's Supper.

The liturgy in its turn moves the faithful, filled with "the paschal sacraments," to be "one in holiness";[19] it prays that "they may hold fast in their lives to what they have grasped by their faith";[20] the renewal in the eucharist of the covenant between the Lord and his people draws the faithful into the compelling love of Christ and sets them on fire. From the liturgy, therefore, particularly the eucharist, grace is poured forth upon us as from a fountain; the liturgy is the source for achieving in the most effective way possible human sanctification and God's glorification, the end to which all the Church's other activities are directed.

11. But in order that the liturgy may possess its full effectiveness, it is necessary that the faithful come to it with proper dispositions, that their minds be attuned to their voices, and that they cooperate with divine grace, lest they receive it in vain.[21] Pastors must therefore realize that when the liturgy is celebrated something more is required than the mere observance of the laws governing valid and lawful celebration; it is also their duty to ensure that the faithful take part fully aware of what they are doing, actively engaged in the rite, and enriched by its effects.

12. The spiritual life, however, is not limited solely to participation in the liturgy. Christians are indeed called to pray in union with each other, but they must also enter into their chamber to pray to the Father in secret;[22] further, according to the teaching of the Apostle, they should pray without ceasing.[23] We learn from the same Apostle that we must always bear about in our body the dying of Jesus, so that the life also of Jesus may be made manifest in our bodily frame.[24] This is why we ask the Lord in the sacrifice of the Mass that "receiving the offering of the spiritual victim," he may fashion us for himself "as an eternal gift."[25]

13. Popular devotions of the Christian people are to be highly endorsed, provided they accord with the laws and norms of the Church, above all when they are ordered by the Apostolic See.

Devotions proper to particular Churches also have a special dignity if they are undertaken by mandate of the bishops according to customs or books lawfully approved.

But these devotions should be so fashioned that they harmonize with the liturgical seasons, accord with the sacred liturgy, are in some way derived from

it, and lead the people to it, since, in fact, the liturgy, by its very nature far surpasses any of them.

II. Promotion of Liturgical Instruction and Active Participation

14. The Church earnestly desires that all the faithful be led to that full, conscious, and active participation in liturgical celebrations called for by the very nature of the liturgy. Such participation by the Christian people as "a chosen race, a royal priesthood, a holy nation, God's own people" (1 Pt. 2:9; see 2:4–5) is their right and duty by reason of their baptism.

In the reform and promotion of the liturgy, this full and active participation by all the people is the aim to be considered before all else. For it is the primary and indispensable source from which the faithful are to derive the true Christian spirit and therefore pastors must zealously strive in all their pastoral work to achieve such participation by means of the necessary instruction.

Yet it would be futile to entertain any hopes of realizing this unless, in the first place, the pastors themselves become thoroughly imbued with the spirit and power of the liturgy and make themselves its teachers. A prime need, therefore, is that attention be directed, first of all, to the liturgical formation of the clergy. Wherefore the Council has decided to enact what follows.

15. Professors appointed to teach liturgy in seminaries, religious houses of study, and theological faculties must be thoroughly trained for their work in institutes specializing in this subject.

16. The study of liturgy is to be ranked among the compulsory and major courses in seminaries and religious houses of studies; in theological faculties it is to rank among the principal courses. It is to be taught under its theological, historical, spiritual, pastoral, and canonical aspects. Moreover, other professors, while striving to expound the mystery of Christ and the history of salvation from the angle proper to each of their own subjects, must nevertheless do so in a way that will clearly bring out the connection between their subjects and the liturgy, as also the underlying unity of all priestly training. This consideration is especially important for professors of dogmatic, spiritual, and pastoral theology and for professors of holy Scripture.

17. In seminaries and houses of religious, clerics shall be given a liturgical formation in their spiritual life. The means for this are: proper guidance so that they may be able to understand the sacred rites and take part in them wholeheartedly; the actual celebration of the sacred mysteries and of other, popular devotions imbued with the spirit of the liturgy. In addition they must learn how to observe the liturgical laws, so that life in seminaries and houses of religious may be thoroughly permeated by the spirit of the liturgy.

18. Priests, both secular and religious, who are already working in the Lord's vineyard are to be helped by every suitable means to understand ever more

fully what it is they are doing in their liturgical functions; they are to be aided to live the liturgical life and to share it with the faithful entrusted to their care.

19. With zeal and patience pastors must promote the liturgical instruction of the faithful and also their active participation in the liturgy both internally and externally, taking into account their age and condition, their way of life, and their stage of religious development. By doing so, pastors will be fulfilling one of their chief duties as faithful stewards of the mysteries of God; and in this matter they must lead their flock not only by word but also by example.

20. Radio and television broadcasts of sacred rites must be marked by discretion and dignity, under the leadership and direction of a competent person appointed for this office by the bishops. This is especially important when the service to be broadcast is the Mass.

III. The Reform of the Sacred Liturgy

21. In order that the Christian people may more surely derive an abundance of graces from the liturgy, the Church desires to undertake with great care a general reform of the liturgy itself. For the liturgy is made up of immutable elements, divinely instituted, and of elements subject to change. These not only may but ought to be changed with the passage of time if they have suffered from the intrusion of anything out of harmony with the inner nature of the liturgy or have become pointless.

In this reform both texts and rites should be so drawn up that they express more clearly the holy things they signify and that the Christian people, as far as possible, are able to understand them with ease and to take part in the rites fully, actively, and as befits a community.

Wherefore the Council establishes the general norms that follow.

A. General Norms

22. §1. Regulation of the liturgy depends solely on the authority of the Church, that is, on the Apostolic See and, accordingly as the law determines, on the bishop.

§2. In virtue of power conceded by the law, the regulation of the liturgy within certain defined limits belongs also to various kinds of competent territorial bodies of bishops lawfully established.

§3. Therefore, no other person, not even if he is a priest, may on his own add, remove, or change anything in the liturgy.

23. That sound tradition may be retained and yet the way remain open to legitimate progress, a careful investigation is always to be made into each part of the liturgy to be revised. This investigation should be theological, historical, and pastoral. Also the general laws governing the structure and meaning of the liturgy must be studied in conjunction with the experience derived

from recent liturgical reforms and from the indults conceded to various places. Finally, there must be no innovations unless the good of the Church genuinely and certainly requires them; care must be taken that any new forms adopted should in some way grow organically from forms already existing.

As far as possible, marked differences between the rites used in neighboring regions must be carefully avoided.

24. Sacred Scripture is of the greatest importance in the celebration of the liturgy. For it is from Scripture that the readings are given and explained in the homily and that psalms are sung; the prayers, collects, and liturgical songs are scriptural in their inspiration; it is from the Scriptures that actions and signs derive their meaning. Thus to achieve the reform, progress, and adaptation of the liturgy, it is essential to promote that warm and living love for Scripture to which the venerable tradition of both Eastern and Western rites gives testimony.

25. The liturgical books are to be revised as soon as possible; experts are to be employed in this task and bishops from various parts of the world are to be consulted.

B. Norms Drawn from the Hierarchic and Communal Nature of the Liturgy

26. Liturgical services are not private functions, but are celebrations belonging to the Church, which is the "sacrament of unity," namely, the holy people united and ordered under their bishops.[26]

Therefore liturgical services involve the whole Body of the Church; they manifest it and have effects upon it; but they also concern the individual members of the Church in different ways, according to their different orders, offices, and actual participation.

27. Whenever rites, according to their specific nature, make provision for communal celebration involving the presence and active participation of the faithful, it is to be stressed that this way of celebrating them is to be preferred, as far as possible, to a celebration that is individual and, so to speak, private.

This applies with special force to the celebration of Mass and the administration of the sacraments, even though every Mass has of itself a public and social character.

28. In liturgical celebrations each one, minister or layperson, who has an office to perform, should do all of, but only, those parts which pertain to that office by the nature of the rite and the principles of liturgy.

29. Servers, readers, commentators, and members of the choir also exercise a genuine liturgical function. They ought to discharge their office, therefore, with the sincere devotion and decorum demanded by so exalted a ministry and rightly expected of them by God's people.

Consequently, they must all be deeply imbued with the spirit of the liturgy, in the measure proper to each one, and they must be trained to perform their functions in a correct and orderly manner.

30. To promote active participation, the people should be encouraged to take part by means of acclamations, responses, psalmody, antiphons, and songs, as well as by actions, gestures, and bearing. And at the proper times all should observe a reverent silence.

31. The revision of the liturgical books must ensure that the rubrics make provision for the parts belonging to the people.

32. The liturgy makes distinctions between persons according to their liturgical function and sacred orders and there are liturgical laws providing for due honors to be given to civil authorities. Apart from these instances, no special honors are to be paid in the liturgy to any private persons or classes of persons, whether in the ceremonies or by external display.

C. *Norms Based on the Teaching and Pastoral Character of the Liturgy*

33. Although the liturgy is above all things the worship of the divine majesty, it likewise contains rich instruction for the faithful.[27] For in the liturgy God is speaking to his people and Christ is still proclaiming his gospel. And the people are responding to God by both song and prayer.

Moreover, the prayers addressed to God by the priest, who presides over the assembly in the person of Christ, are said in the name of the entire holy people and of all present. And the visible signs used by the liturgy to signify invisible divine realities have been chosen by Christ or the Church. Thus not only when things are read "that were written for our instruction" (Rom 15:4), but also when the Church prays or sings or acts, the faith of those taking part is nourished and their minds are raised to God, so that they may offer him their worship as intelligent beings and receive his grace more abundantly.

In the reform of the liturgy, therefore, the following general norms are to be observed.

34. The rites should be marked by a noble simplicity; they should be short, clear, and unencumbered by useless repetitions; they should be within the people's powers of comprehension and as a rule not require much explanation.

35. That the intimate connection between words and rites may stand out clearly in the liturgy:

1. In sacred celebrations there is to be more reading from holy Scripture and it is to be more varied and apposite.

2. Because the spoken word is part of the liturgical service, the best place for it, consistent with the nature of the rite, is to be indicated even in the rubrics; the ministry of preaching is to be fulfilled with exactitude and fidelity. Preaching should draw its content mainly from scriptural and liturgical

sources, being a proclamation of God's wonderful works in the history of salvation, the mystery of Christ, ever present and active within us, especially in the celebration of the liturgy.

3. A more explicitly liturgical catechesis should also be given in a variety of ways. Within the rites themselves provision is to be made for brief comments, when needed, by the priest or a qualified minister; they should occur only at the more suitable moments and use a set formula or something similar.

4. Bible services should be encouraged, especially on the vigils of the more solemn feasts, on some weekdays in Advent and Lent, and on Sundays and holy days. They are particularly to be recommended in places where no priest is available; when this is the case, a deacon or some other person authorized by the bishop is to preside over the celebration.

36. §1. Particular law remaining in force, the use of the Latin language is to be preserved in the Latin rites.

§2. But since the use of the mother tongue, whether in the Mass, the administration of the sacraments, or other parts of the liturgy, frequently may be of great advantage to the people, the limits of its use may be extended. This will apply in the first place to the readings and instructions and to some prayers and chants, according to the regulations on this matter to be laid down for each case in subsequent chapters.

§3. Respecting such norms and also, where applicable, consulting the bishops of nearby territories of the same language, the competent, territorial ecclesiastical authority mentioned in art. 22, §2 is empowered to decide whether and to what extent the vernacular is to be used. The enactments of the competent authority are to be approved, that is, confirmed by the Holy See.

§4. Translations from the Latin text into the mother tongue intended for use in the liturgy must be approved by the competent, territorial ecclesiastical authority already mentioned.

D. Norms for Adapting the Liturgy to the Culture and Traditions of Peoples

37. Even in the liturgy the Church has no wish to impose a rigid uniformity in matters that do not affect the faith or the good of the whole community; rather, the Church respects and fosters the genius and talents of the various races and peoples. The Church considers with sympathy and, if possible, preserves intact the elements in these peoples' way of life that are not indissolubly bound up with superstition and error. Sometimes in fact the Church admits such elements into the liturgy itself, provided they are in keeping with the true and authentic spirit of the liturgy.

38. Provisions shall also be made, even in the revision of liturgical books, for legitimate variations and adaptations to different groups, regions, and peoples, especially in mission lands, provided the substantial unity of the Roman Rite is preserved; this should be borne in mind when rites are drawn up and rubrics devised.

39. Within the limits set by the editio typica of the liturgical books, it shall be for the competent, territorial ecclesiastical authority mentioned in art. 22, §2 to specify adaptations, especially in the case of the administration of the sacraments, the sacramentals, processions, liturgical language, sacred music, and the arts. This, however, is to be done in accord with the fundamental norms laid down in this Constitution.

40. In some places and circumstances, however, an even more radical adaptation of the liturgy is needed and this entails greater difficulties. Wherefore:

    1. The competent, territorial ecclesiastical authority mentioned in art. 22, §2, must, in this matter, carefully and prudently weigh what elements from the traditions and culture of individual peoples may be appropriately admitted into divine worship. They are to propose to the Apostolic See adaptations considered useful or necessary that will be introduced with its consent.

    2. To ensure that adaptations are made with all the circumspection they demand, the Apostolic See will grant power to this same territorial ecclesiastical authority to permit and to direct, as the case requires, the necessary preliminary experiments within certain groups suited for the purpose and for a fixed time.

    3. Because liturgical laws often involve special difficulties with respect to adaptation, particularly in mission lands, experts in these matters must be employed to formulate them.

IV. Promotion of Liturgical Life in Diocese and Parish

41. The bishop is to be looked on as the high priest of his flock, the faithful's life in Christ in some way deriving from and depending on him.

Therefore all should hold in great esteem the liturgical life of the diocese centered around the bishop, especially in his cathedral church; they must be convinced that the preeminent manifestation of the Church is present in the full, active participation of all God's holy people in these liturgical celebrations, especially in the same eucharist, in a single prayer, at one altar at which the bishop presides, surrounded by his college of priests and by his ministers.[28]

42. But because it is impossible for the bishop always and everywhere to preside over the whole flock in his Church, he cannot do otherwise than establish lesser groupings of the faithful. Among these the parishes, set up locally under a pastor taking the place of the bishop, are the most important: in some manner they represent the visible Church established throughout the world.

And therefore both in attitude and in practice the liturgical life of the parish and its relationship to the bishop must be fostered among the faithful and clergy; efforts must also be made toward a lively sense of community within the parish, above all in the shared celebration of the Sunday Mass.

V. Promotion of Pastoral-Liturgical Action

43. Zeal for the promotion and restoration of the liturgy is rightly held to be a sign of the providential dispositions of God in our time, a movement of the Holy Spirit in his Church. Today it is a distinguishing mark of the Church's life, indeed of the whole tenor of contemporary religious thought and action.

So that this pastoral-liturgical action may become even more vigorous in the Church, the Council decrees what follows.

44. It is advisable that the competent, territorial ecclesiastical authority mentioned in art. 22, §2 set up a liturgical commission, to be assisted by experts in liturgical science, music, art, and pastoral practice. As far as possible the commission should be aided by some kind of institute for pastoral liturgy, consisting of persons eminent in these matters and including the laity as circumstances suggest. Under the direction of the aforementioned territorial ecclesiastical authority, the commission is to regulate pastoral-liturgical action throughout the territory and to promote studies and necessary experiments whenever there is question of adaptations to be proposed to the Apostolic See.

45. For the same reason every diocese is to have a commission on the liturgy, under the direction of the bishop, for promoting the liturgical apostolate.

Sometimes it may be advisable for several dioceses to form among themselves one single commission, in order to promote the liturgy by means of shared consultation.

46. Besides the commission on the liturgy, every diocese, as far as possible, should have commissions for music and art.

These three commissions must work in closest collaboration; indeed it will often be best to fuse the three of them into one single commission.

Chapter II
The Most Sacred Mystery of the Eucharist

47. At the Last Supper, on the night when he was betrayed, our Savior instituted the eucharistic sacrifice of his body and blood. He did this in order to perpetuate the sacrifice of the cross throughout the centuries until he should come again and in this way to entrust to his beloved Bride, the Church, a memorial of his death and resurrection: a sacrament of love, a sign of unity, a bond of charity,[1] a paschal banquet "in which Christ is eaten, the heart is filled with grace, and a pledge of future glory given to us."[2]

48. The Church, therefore, earnestly desires that Christ's faithful, when present at this mystery of faith, should not be there as strangers or silent spectators; on the contrary, through a good understanding of the rites and prayers they should take part in the sacred service conscious of what they are doing, with devotion and full involvement. They should be instructed by God's word and be nourished at the table of the Lord's body; they should give thanks to God; by offering the immaculate Victim, not only through the hands of the priest, but also with him, they should learn to offer themselves as well; through Christ the Mediator,[3] they should be formed day by day into an ever more perfect unity with God and with each other, so that finally God may be all in all.

49. Thus, mindful of those Masses celebrated with the assistance of the faithful, especially on Sundays and holy days of obligation, the Council makes the following decrees in order that the sacrifice of the Mass, even in its ritual forms, may become pastorally effective to the utmost degree.

50. The Order of Mass is to be revised in a way that will bring out more clearly the intrinsic nature and purpose of its several parts, as also the connection between them, and will more readily achieve the devout, active participation of the faithful.

For this purpose the rites are to be simplified, due care being taken to preserve their substance; elements that, with the passage of time, came to be duplicated or were added with but little advantage are now to be discarded; other elements that have suffered injury through accident of history are now, as may seem useful or necessary, to be restored to the vigor they had in the traditions of the Fathers.

51. The treasures of the Bible are to be opened up more lavishly, so that a richer share in God's word may be provided for the faithful. In this way a more representative portion of holy Scripture will be read to the people in the course of a prescribed number of years.

52. By means of the homily the mysteries of the faith and the guiding principles of the Christian life are expounded from the sacred text during the course of the liturgical year; as part of the liturgy itself therefore, the homily is strongly recommended; in fact, at Masses celebrated with the assistance of the people on Sundays and holy days of obligation it is not to be omitted except for a serious reason.

53. Especially on Sundays and holy days of obligation there is to be restored, after the gospel and the homily, "the universal prayer" or "the prayer of the faithful." By this prayer, in which the people are to take part, intercession shall be made for holy Church, for the civil authorities, for those oppressed by various needs, for all people, and for the salvation of the entire world.[4]

54. With art. 36 of this Constitution as the norm, in Masses celebrated with the people a suitable place may be allotted to their mother tongue. This is to

apply in the first place to the readings and "the universal prayer," but also, as local conditions may warrant, to those parts belonging to the people.

Nevertheless steps should be taken enabling the faithful to say or to sing together in Latin those parts of the Ordinary of the Mass belonging to them.

Wherever a more extended use of the mother tongue within the Mass appears desirable, the regulation laid down in art. 40 of this Constitution is to be observed.

55. That more complete form of participation in the Mass by which the faithful, after the priest's communion, receive the Lord's body from the sacrifice, is strongly endorsed.

The dogmatic principles laid down by the Council of Trent remain intact.[5] In instances to be specified by the Apostolic See, however, communion under both kinds may be granted both to clerics and religious and to the laity at the discretion of the bishops, for example, to the ordained at the Mass of their ordination, to the professed at the Mass of their religious profession, to the newly baptized at the Mass following their baptism.

56. The two parts that, in a certain sense, go to make up the Mass, namely, the liturgy of the word and the liturgy of the eucharist, are so closely connected with each other that they form but one single act of worship. Accordingly this Council strongly urges pastors that in their catechesis they insistently teach the faithful to take part in the entire Mass, especially on Sundays and holy days of obligation.

57. §1. Concelebration, which aptly expresses the unity of the priesthood, has continued to this day as a practice in the Church of both East and West. For this reason it has seemed good to the Council to extend permission for concelebration to the following cases:

> 1. a. on Holy Thursday, both the chrism Mass and the evening Mass;
> b. Masses during councils, bishops' conferences, and synods;
> c. the Mass at the blessing of an abbot.

> 2. Also, with permission of the Ordinary, who is the one to decide whether concelebration is opportune, to:
> a. the conventual Mass and the principal Mass in churches, when the needs of the faithful do not require that all the priests on hand celebrate individually;
> b. Masses celebrated at any kind of meeting of priests, whether secular or religious.

> §2. 1. The regulation, however, of the discipline of concelebration in the diocese pertains to the bishop.

> 2. This, however, does not take away the option of every priest to celebrate Mass individually, not, however, at the same time and in the same church as a concelebrated Mass or on Holy Thursday.

58. A new rite for concelebration is to be drawn up and inserted into the Roman Pontifical and Roman Missal.

Chapter III
The Other Sacraments and the Sacramentals

59. The purpose of the sacraments is to make people holy, to build up the Body of Christ, and, finally, to give worship to God; but being signs they also have a teaching function. They not only presuppose faith, but by words and objects they also nourish, strengthen, and express it; that is why they are called "sacraments of faith." They do indeed impart grace, but, in addition, the very act of celebrating them disposes the faithful most effectively to receive this grace in a fruitful manner, to worship God rightly, and to practice charity.

It is therefore of the highest importance that the faithful should readily understand the sacramental signs and should with great eagerness frequent those sacraments that were instituted to nourish the Christian life.

60. The Church has, in addition, instituted sacramentals. These are sacred signs bearing a kind of resemblance to the sacraments: they signify effects, particularly of a spiritual kind, that are obtained through the Church's intercession. They dispose people to receive the chief effect of the sacraments and they make holy various occasions in human life.

61. Thus, for well-disposed members of the faithful, the effect of the liturgy of the sacraments and sacramentals is that almost every event in their lives is made holy by divine grace that flows from the paschal mystery of Christ's passion, death, and resurrection, the fount from which all sacraments and sacramentals draw their power. The liturgy means also that there is hardly any proper use of material things that cannot thus be directed toward human sanctification and the praise of God.

62. With the passage of time, however, certain features have crept into the rites of the sacraments and sacramentals that have made their nature and purpose less clear to the people of today; hence some changes have become necessary as adaptations to the needs of our own times. For this reason the Council decrees what follows concerning the revision of these rites.

63. Because the use of the mother tongue in the administration of the sacraments and sacramentals can often be of considerable help for the people, this use is to be extended according to the following norms:

a. With art. 36 as the norm, the vernacular may be used in administering the sacraments and sacramentals.

b. Particular rituals in harmony with the new edition of the Roman Ritual shall be prepared without delay by the competent, territorial ecclesiastical authority mentioned in art. 22, §2 of this Constitution. These rituals are to be adapted, even in regard to the language employed, to the needs of the different

regions. Once they have been reviewed by the Apostolic See, they are to be used in the regions for which they have been prepared. But those who draw up these rituals or particular collections of rites must not leave out the prefatory instructions for the individual rites in the Roman Ritual, whether the instructions are pastoral and rubrical or have some special social bearing.

64. The catechumenate for adults, divided into several stages, is to be restored and put into use at the discretion of the local Ordinary. By this means the time of the catechumenate, which is intended as a period of well-suited instruction, may be sanctified by sacred rites to be celebrated at successive intervals of time.

65. With art. 37–40 of this Constitution as the norm, it is lawful in mission lands to allow, besides what is part of Christian tradition, those initiation elements in use among individual peoples, to the extent that such elements are compatible with the Christian rite of initiation.

66. Both of the rites for the baptism of adults are to be revised: not only the simpler rite, but also the more solemn one, with proper attention to the restored catechumenate. A special Mass "On the Occasion of a Baptism" is to be incorporated into the Roman Missal.

67. The rite for the baptism of infants is to be revised and it should be suited to the fact that those to be baptized are infants. The roles as well as the obligations of parents and godparents should be brought out more clearly in the rite itself.

68. The baptismal rite should contain alternatives, to be used at the discretion of the local Ordinary, for occasions when a very large number are to be baptized together. Moreover, a shorter rite is to be drawn up, especially in mission lands, for use by catechists, but also by the faithful in general, when there is danger of death and neither a priest nor a deacon is available.

69. In place of the rite called the "Order of Supplying What Was Omitted in the Baptism of an Infant," a new rite is to be drawn up. This should manifest more clearly and fittingly that an infant who was baptized by the short rite has already been received into the Church.

Similarly, a new rite is to be drawn up for converts who have already been validly baptized; it should express that they are being received into the communion of the Church.

70. Except during the Easter season, baptismal water may be blessed within the rite of baptism itself by use of an approved, shorter formulary.

71. The rite of confirmation is also to be revised in order that the intimate connection of this sacrament with the whole of Christian initiation may stand out more clearly; for this reason it is fitting for candidates to renew their baptismal promises just before they are confirmed.

Confirmation may be conferred within Mass when convenient; as for the rite outside Mass, a formulary is to be composed for use as an introduction.

72. The rite and formularies for the sacrament of penance are to be revised so that they more clearly express both the nature and effect of the sacrament.

73. "Extreme unction," which may also and more properly be called "anointing of the sick," is not a sacrament for those only who are at the point of death. Hence, as soon as any one of the faithful begins to be in danger of death from sickness or old age, the fitting time for that person to receive this sacrament has certainly already arrived.

74. In addition to the separate rites for anointing of the sick and for viaticum, a continuous rite shall be drawn up, structured so that the sick person is anointed after confessing and before receiving viaticum.

75. The number of the anointings is to be adapted to the circumstances; the prayers that belong to the rite of anointing are to be so revised that they correspond to the varying conditions of the sick who receive the sacrament.

76. Both the ceremonies and texts of the ordination rites are to be revised. The address given by the bishop at the beginning of each ordination or consecration may be in the vernacular.

When a bishop is consecrated, all the bishops present may take part in the laying on of hands.

77. The marriage rite now found in the Roman Ritual is to be revised and enriched in such a way that it more clearly signifies the grace of the sacrament and imparts a knowledge of the obligations of spouses.

"If any regions follow other praiseworthy customs and ceremonies when celebrating the sacrament of marriage, the Council earnestly desires that by all means these be retained."[1]

Moreover, the competent, territorial ecclesiastical authority mentioned in art. 22, §2 of this Constitution is free to draw up, in accord with art. 63, its own rite, suited to the usages of place and people. But the rite must always conform to the law that the priest assisting at the marriage must ask for and obtain the consent of the contracting parties.

78. Marriage is normally to be celebrated within Mass, after the reading of the gospel and the homily and before "the prayer of the faithful." The prayer for the bride, duly emended to remind both spouses of their equal obligation to remain faithful to each other, may be said in the vernacular.

But if the sacrament of marriage is celebrated apart from Mass, the epistle and gospel from the nuptial Mass are to be read at the beginning of the rite and the blessing is always to be given to the spouses.

79. The sacramentals are to be reviewed in the light of the primary criterion that the faithful participate intelligently, actively, and easily; the conditions of

our own days must also be considered. When rituals are revised, in accord with art. 63, new sacramentals may also be added as the need for them becomes apparent.

Reserved blessings shall be very few; reservations shall be in favor only of bishops and Ordinaries.

Let provision be made that some sacramentals, at least in special circumstances and at the discretion of the Ordinary, may be administered by qualified laypersons.

80. The rite for the consecration to a life of virginity as it exists in the Roman Pontifical is to be revised.

A rite of religious profession and renewal of vows shall be drawn up with a view to achieving greater unity, simplicity, and dignity. Apart from exceptions in particular law, this rite should be adopted by those who make their profession or renewal of vows within Mass.

Religious profession should preferably be made within Mass.

81. The rite of funerals should express more clearly the paschal character of Christian death and should correspond more closely to the circumstances and traditions of various regions. This applies also to the liturgical color to be used.

82. The rite for the burial of infants is to be revised and a special Mass for the occasion provided.

Chapter IV
Divine Office

83. Christ Jesus, High Priest of the new and eternal covenant, taking human nature, introduced into this earthly exile the hymn that is sung throughout all ages in the halls of heaven. He joins the entire human community to himself, associating it with his own singing of this canticle of divine praise.

For he continues his priestly work through the agency of his Church, which is unceasingly engaged in praising the Lord and interceding for the salvation of the whole world. The Church does this not only by celebrating the eucharist, but also in other ways, especially by praying the divine office.

84. By tradition going back to early Christian times, the divine office is so arranged that the whole course of the day and night is made holy by the praises of God. Therefore, when this wonderful song of praise is rightly performed by priests and others who are deputed for this purpose by the Church's ordinance or by the faithful praying together with the priest in the approved form, then it is truly the voice of a bride addressing her bridegroom; it is the very prayer that Christ himself, together with his Body, addresses to the Father.

85. Hence all who render this service are not only fulfilling a duty of the Church, but also are sharing in the greatest honor of Christ's Bride, for by

offering these praises to God they are standing before God's throne in the name of the Church, their Mother.

86. Priests engaged in the sacred pastoral ministry will offer the praises of the hours with greater fervor the more vividly they realize that they must heed St. Paul's exhortation: "Pray without ceasing" (1 Thes 5:17). For the work in which they labor will effect nothing and bring forth no fruit except by the power of the Lord who said: "Without me you can do nothing" (Jn 15:5). That is why the apostles, instituting deacons, said: "We will devote ourselves to prayer and to the ministry of the word" (Acts 6:4).

87. In order that the divine office may be better and more completely carried out in existing circumstances, whether by priests or by other members of the Church, the Council, carrying further the restoration already so happily begun by the Apostolic See, has seen fit to decree what follows concerning the office of the Roman Rite.

88. Because the purpose of the office is to sanctify the day, the traditional sequence of the hours is to be restored so that once again they may be genuinely related to the hour of the day when they are prayed, as far as it is possible. Moreover, it will be necessary to take into account the modern conditions in which daily life has to be lived, especially by those who are called to labor in apostolic works.

89. Therefore, when the office is revised, these norms are to be observed:
    a. By the venerable tradition of the universal Church, lauds as morning prayer and vespers as evening prayer are the two hinges on which the daily office turns; hence they are to be considered as the chief hours and celebrated as such.
    b. Compline is to be so composed that it will be a suitable prayer for the end of the day.
    c. The hour known as matins, although it should retain the character of nocturnal praise when celebrated in choir, shall be adapted so that it may be recited at any hour of the day; it shall be made up of fewer psalms and longer readings.
    d. The hour of prime is to be suppressed.
    e. In choir the minor hours of terce, sext, and none are to be observed. But outside choir it will be lawful to choose whichever of the three best suits the hour of the day.

90. The divine office, because it is the public prayer of the Church, is a source of devotion and nourishment also for personal prayer. Therefore priests and all others who take part in the divine office are earnestly exhorted in the Lord to attune their minds to their voices when praying it. The better to achieve this, let them take steps to improve their understanding of the liturgy and of the Bible, especially the psalms.

In revising the Roman office, its ancient and venerable treasures are to be so adapted that all those to whom they are handed on may more fully and readily draw profit from them.

91. So that it may really be possible in practice to observe the course of the hours proposed in art. 89, the psalms are no longer to be distributed over just one week, but over some longer period of time.

The work of revising the psalter, already happily begun, is to be finished as soon as possible and is to take into account the style of Christian Latin, the liturgical use of psalms, including their being sung, and the entire tradition of the Latin Church.

92. As regards the readings, the following shall be observed:

  a. Readings from sacred Scripture shall be arranged so that the riches of God's word may be easily accessible in more abundant measure.

  b. Readings excerpted from the works of the Fathers, doctors, and ecclesiastical writers shall be better selected.

  c. The accounts of the martyrdom or lives of the saints are to be made to accord with the historical facts.

93. To whatever extent may seem advisable, the hymns are to be restored to their original form and any allusion to mythology or anything that conflicts with Christian piety is to be dropped or changed. Also, as occasion arises, let other selections from the treasury of hymns be incorporated.

94. That the day may be truly sanctified and the hours themselves recited with spiritual advantage, it is best that each of them be prayed at a time most closely corresponding to the true time of each canonical hour.

95. In addition to the conventual Mass, communities obliged to choral office are bound to celebrate the office in choir every day. In particular:

  a. Orders of canons, of monks and of nuns, and of other regulars bound by law or constitutions to choral office must celebrate the entire office.

  b. Cathedral or collegiate chapters are bound to recite those parts of the office imposed on them by general or particular law.

  c. All members of the above communities who are in major orders or are solemnly professed, except for lay brothers, are bound individually to recite those canonical hours which they do not pray in choir.

96. Clerics not bound to office in choir, if they are in major orders, are bound to pray the entire office every day, either in common or individually, following the norms in art. 89.

97. Appropriate instances are to be defined by the rubrics in which a liturgical service may be substituted for the divine office.

In particular cases and for a just reason Ordinaries may dispense their subjects wholly or in part from the obligation of reciting the divine office or may commute it.

98. Members of any institute dedicated to acquiring perfection who, according to their constitutions, are to recite any parts of the divine office are thereby performing the public prayer of the Church.

They too perform the public prayer of the Church who, in virtue of their constitutions, recite any little office, provided this has been drawn up after the pattern of the divine office and duly approved.

99. Since the divine office is the voice of the Church, that is, of the whole Mystical Body publicly praising God, those clerics who are not obliged to office in choir, especially priests who live together or who meet together for any purpose, are urged to pray at least some part of the divine office in common.

All who pray the divine office, whether in choir or in common, should fulfill the task entrusted to them as perfectly as possible: this refers not only to the internal devotion of their minds but also to their external manner of celebration.

It is advantageous, moreover, that the office in choir and in common be sung when there is an opportunity to do so.

100. Pastors should see to it that the chief hours, especially vespers, are celebrated in common in church on Sundays and the more solemn feasts. The laity, too, are encouraged to recite the divine office either with the priests, or among themselves, or even individually.

101. §1. In accordance with the centuries-old tradition of the Latin rite, clerics are to retain the Latin language in the divine office. But in individual cases the Ordinary has the power of granting the use of a vernacular translation, prepared in accord with art. 36, to those clerics for whom the use of Latin constitutes a grave obstacle to their praying the office properly.

§2. The competent superior has the power to grant the use of the vernacular in the celebration of the divine office, even in choir, to nuns and to members of institutes dedicated to acquiring perfection, both men who are not clerics and women. The version, however, must be one that has been approved.

§3. Any cleric bound to the divine office fulfills his obligation if he prays the office in the vernacular together with a group of the faithful or with those mentioned in §2, provided the text of the translation has been approved.

Chapter V
The Liturgical Year

102. The Church is conscious that it must celebrate the saving work of the divine Bridegroom by devoutly recalling it on certain days throughout the course of the year. Every week, on the day which the Church has called the Lord's Day, it keeps the memory of the Lord's resurrection, which it also

celebrates once in the year, together with his blessed passion, in the most solemn festival of Easter.

Within the cycle of a year, moreover, the Church unfolds the whole mystery of Christ, from his incarnation and birth until his ascension, the day of Pentecost, and the expectation of blessed hope and of the Lord's return.

Recalling thus the mysteries of redemption, the Church opens to the faithful the riches of the Lord's powers and merits, so that these are in some way made present in every age in order that the faithful may lay hold on them and be filled with saving grace.

103. In celebrating this annual cycle of Christ's mysteries, the Church honors with special love Mary, the Mother of God, who is joined by an inseparable bond to the saving work of her Son. In her the Church holds up and admires the most excellent effect of the redemption and joyfully contemplates, as in a flawless image, that which the Church itself desires and hopes wholly to be.

104. The Church has also included in the annual cycle days devoted to the memory of the martyrs and the other saints. Raised up to perfection by the manifold grace of God and already in possession of eternal salvation, they sing God's perfect praise in heaven and offer prayers for us. By celebrating their passage from earth to heaven the Church proclaims the paschal mystery achieved in the saints, who have suffered and been glorified with Christ; it proposes them to the faithful as examples drawing all to the Father through Christ and pleads through their merits for God's favors.

105. Finally, in the various seasons of the year and according to its traditional discipline, the Church completes the formation of the faithful by means of devout practices for soul and body, by instruction, prayer, and works of penance and of mercy.

Accordingly the sacred Council has seen fit to decree what follows.

106. By a tradition handed down from the apostles and having its origin from the very day of Christ's resurrection, the Church celebrates the paschal mystery every eighth day, which, with good reason, bears the name of the Lord's Day or Sunday. For on this day Christ's faithful must gather together so that, by hearing the word of God and taking part in the eucharist, they may call to mind the passion, the resurrection, and the glorification of the Lord Jesus and may thank God, who "has begotten them again unto a living hope through the resurrection of Jesus Christ from the dead" (1 Pt. 1:3). Hence the Lord's Day is the first holy day of all and should be proposed to the devotion of the faithful and taught to them in such a way that it may become in fact a day of joy and of freedom from work. Other celebrations, unless they be truly of greatest importance, shall not have precedence over the Sunday, the foundation and core of the whole liturgical year.

107. The liturgical year is to be so revised that the traditional customs and usages of the sacred seasons are preserved or restored to suit the conditions

of modern times; their specific character is to be retained, so that they duly nourish the devotion of the faithful who celebrate the mysteries of Christian redemption and above all the paschal mystery. If certain adaptations are considered necessary on account of local conditions, they are to be made in accordance with the provisions of art. 39 and 40.

108. The minds of the faithful must be directed primarily toward those feasts of the Lord on which the mysteries of salvation are celebrated in the course of the year. Therefore, the Proper of Seasons shall be given the precedence due to it over the feasts of the saints, in order that the entire cycle of the mysteries of salvation may be celebrated in the measure due to them.

109. Lent is marked by two themes, the baptismal and the penitential. By recalling or preparing for baptism and by repentance, this season disposes the faithful, as they more diligently listen to the word of God and devote themselves to prayer, to celebrate the paschal mystery. The baptismal and penitential aspects of Lent are to be given greater prominence in both the liturgy and liturgical catechesis. Hence:

a. More use is to be made of the baptismal features proper to the Lenten liturgy; some of those from an earlier era are to be restored as may seem advisable.

b. The same is to apply to the penitential elements. As regards catechesis, it is important to impress on the minds of the faithful not only the social consequences of sin but also the essence of the virtue of penance, namely, detestation of sin as an offense against God; the role of the Church in penitential practices is not to be neglected and the people are to be exhorted to pray for sinners.

110. During Lent penance should be not only inward and individual, but also outward and social. The practice of penance should be fostered, however, in ways that are possible in our own times and in different regions and according to the circumstances of the faithful; it should be encouraged by the authorities mentioned in art. 22.

Nevertheless, let the paschal fast be kept sacred. Let it be observed everywhere on Good Friday and, where possible, prolonged throughout Holy Saturday, as a way of coming to the joys of the Sunday of the resurrection with uplifted and welcoming heart.

111. The saints have been traditionally honored in the Church and their authentic relics and images held in veneration. For the feasts of the saints proclaim the wonderful works of Christ in his servants and display to the faithful fitting examples for their imitation.

Lest the feasts of the saints take precedence over the feasts commemorating the very mysteries of salvation, many of them should be left to be celebrated by a particular Church or nation or religious family; those only should

be extended to the universal Church that commemorate saints of truly universal significance.

Chapter VI
Sacred Music

112. The musical tradition of the universal Church is a treasure of inestimable value, greater even than that of any other art. The main reason for this preeminence is that, as sacred song closely bound to the text, it forms a necessary or integral part of the solemn liturgy.

Holy Scripture itself has bestowed praise upon sacred song[1] and the same may be said of the Fathers of the Church and of the Roman pontiffs, who in recent times, led by St. Pius X, have explained more precisely the ministerial function supplied by sacred music in the service of the Lord.

Therefore sacred music will be the more holy the more closely it is joined to the liturgical rite, whether by adding delight to prayer, fostering oneness of spirit, or investing the rites with greater solemnity. But the Church approves of all forms of genuine art possessing the qualities required and admits them into divine worship.

Accordingly, the Council, keeping the norms and precepts of ecclesiastical tradition and discipline and having regard to the purpose of sacred music, which is the glory of God and the sanctification of the faithful, decrees what follows.

113. A liturgical service takes on a nobler aspect when the rites are celebrated with singing, the sacred ministers take their parts in them, and the faithful actively participate.

As regards the language to be used, the provisions of art. 36 are to be observed; for the Mass, those of art. 54; for the sacraments, those of art. 63; for the divine office, those of art. 101.

114. The treasure of sacred music is to be preserved and fostered with great care. Choirs must be diligently developed, especially in cathedral churches; but bishops and other pastors of souls must be at pains to ensure that whenever a liturgical service is to be celebrated with song, the whole assembly of the faithful is enabled, in keeping with art. 28 and 30, to contribute the active participation that rightly belongs to it.

115. Great importance is to be attached to the teaching and practice of music in seminaries, in the novitiates and houses of study of religious of both sexes, and also in other Catholic institutions and schools. To impart this instruction, those in charge of teaching sacred music are to receive thorough training.

It is recommended also that higher institutes of sacred music be established whenever possible.

Musicians and singers, especially young boys, must also be given a genuine liturgical training.

116. The Church acknowledges Gregorian chant as distinctive of the Roman liturgy; therefore, other things being equal, it should be given pride of place in liturgical services.

But other kinds of sacred music, especially polyphony, are by no means excluded from liturgical celebrations, provided they accord with the spirit of the liturgical service, in the way laid down in art. 30.

117. The editio typica of the books of Gregorian chant is to be completed and a more critical edition is to be prepared of those books already published since the reform of St. Pius X.

It is desirable also that an edition be prepared containing the simpler melodies for use in small churches.

118. The people's own religious songs are to be encouraged with care so that in sacred devotions as well as during services of the liturgy itself, in keeping with rubrical norms and requirements, the faithful may raise their voices in song.

119. In certain parts of the world, especially mission lands, people have their own musical traditions and these play a great part in their religious and social life. Thus, in keeping with art. 39 and 40, due importance is to be attached to their music and a suitable place given to it, not only in forming their attitude toward religion, but also in adapting worship to their native genius.

Therefore, when missionaries are being given training in music, every effort should be made to see that they become competent in promoting the traditional music of the people, both in schools and in sacred services, as far as may be practicable.

120. In the Latin Church the pipe organ is to be held in high esteem, for it is the traditional musical instrument that adds a wonderful splendor to the Church's ceremonies and powerfully lifts up the spirit to God and to higher things.

But other instruments also may be admitted for use in divine worship, with the knowledge and consent of the competent territorial authority and in conformity with art. 22, §2, art. 37 and art. 40. This applies, however, only on condition that the instruments are suitable, or can be made suitable, for sacred use, are in accord with the dignity of the place of worship, and truly contribute to the uplifting of the faithful.

121. Composers, filled with the Christian spirit, should feel that their vocation is to develop sacred music and to increase its store of treasures.

Let them produce compositions having the qualities proper to genuine sacred music, not confining themselves to works that can be sung only by

large choirs, but providing also for the needs of small choirs and for the active participation of the entire assembly of the faithful.

The texts intended to be sung must always be consistent with Catholic teaching; indeed they should be drawn chiefly from holy Scripture and from liturgical sources.

Chapter VII
Sacred Art and Sacred Furnishings

122. The fine arts are deservedly ranked among the noblest activities of human genius and this applies especially to religious art and to its highest achievement, sacred art. These arts, by their very nature, are oriented toward the infinite beauty of God, which they attempt in some way to portray by the work of human hands. They are dedicated to advancing God's praise and glory to the degree that they center on the single aim of turning the human spirit devoutly toward God.

The Church has therefore always been the friend of the fine arts, has ever sought their noble help, and has trained artists with the special aim that all things set apart for use in divine worship are truly worthy, becoming, and beautiful, signs and symbols of the supernatural world. The Church has always regarded itself as the rightful arbiter of the arts, deciding which of the works of artists are in accordance with faith, with reverence, and with honored traditional laws and are thereby suited for sacred use.

The Church has been particularly careful to see that sacred furnishings worthily and beautifully serve the dignity of worship and has admitted changes in materials, design, or ornamentation prompted by the progress of the technical arts with the passage of time.

Wherefore it has pleased the Fathers to issue the following decrees on these matters.

123. The Church has not adopted any particular style of art as its very own but has admitted styles from every period, according to the proper genius and circumstances of peoples and the requirements of the many different rites in the Church. Thus, in the course of the centuries, the Church has brought into being a treasury of art that must be very carefully preserved. The art of our own days, coming from every race and region, shall also be given free scope in the Church, on condition that it serves the places of worship and sacred rites with the reverence and honor due to them. In this way contemporary art can add its own voice to that wonderful chorus of praise sung by the great masters of past ages of Catholic faith.

124. In encouraging and favoring art that is truly sacred, Ordinaries should strive after noble beauty rather than mere sumptuous display. This principle is to apply also in the matter of sacred vestments and appointments.

Let bishops carefully remove from the house of God and from other places of worship those works of artists that are repugnant to faith and morals and to Christian devotion and that offend true religious sense either by their grotesqueness or by the deficiency, mediocrity, or sham in their artistic quality.

When churches are to be built, let great care be taken that they are well suited to celebrating liturgical services and to bringing about the active participation of the faithful.

125. The practice of placing sacred images in churches so that they may be venerated by the faithful is to be maintained. Nevertheless there is to be restraint regarding their number and prominence so that they do not create confusion among the Christian people or foster religious practices of doubtful orthodoxy.

126. When deciding on works of art, local Ordinaries shall give hearing to the diocesan commission on sacred art, and if need be, to others who are especially expert, as well as to the commissions referred to in art. 44, 45, and 46. Ordinaries must be very careful to see that sacred furnishings and valuable works of art are not disposed of or damaged, for they are the adornment of the house of God.

127. Bishops should have a special concern for artists, so as to imbue them with the spirit of sacred art and liturgy. This they may do in person or through competent priests who are gifted with a knowledge and love of art.

It is also recommended that schools or academies of sacred art to train artists be founded in those parts of the world where they seem useful.

All artists who, prompted by their talents, desire to serve God's glory in holy Church, should ever bear in mind that they are engaged in a kind of sacred imitation of God the Creator and are concerned with works intended to be used in Catholic worship, to uplift the faithful, and to foster their devotion and religious formation.

128. Along with the revision of the liturgical books, as laid down in art. 25, there is to be an early revision of the canons and ecclesiastical statutes regulating the supplying of material things involved in sacred worship. This applies in particular to the worthy and well-planned construction of places of worship, the design and construction of altars, the nobility, placement, and security of the eucharistic tabernacle, the practicality and dignity of the baptistry, the appropriate arrangement of sacred images and church decorations and appointments. Laws that seem less suited to the reformed liturgy are to be brought into harmony with it or else abolished; laws that are helpful are to be retained if already in use or introduced where they are lacking.

With art. 22 of this Constitution as the norm, the territorial bodies of bishops are empowered to make adaptations to the needs and customs of their different regions; this applies especially to the material and design of sacred furnishings and vestments.

129. During their philosophical and theological studies, clerics are to be taught about the history and development of sacred art and about the sound principles on which the production of its works must be grounded. In consequence they will be able to appreciate and preserve the Church's treasured monuments and be in a position to offer good advice to artists who are engaged in producing works of art.

130. It is fitting that the use of pontifical insignia be reserved to those ecclesiastical persons who have either episcopal rank or some definite jurisdiction.

Appendix
Declaration of the Second Vatican Ecumenical Council on Revision of the Calendar

131. The Second Vatican Ecumenical Council recognizes the importance of the wishes expressed by many on assigning the feast of Easter to a fixed Sunday and on an unchanging calendar and has considered the effects that could result from the introduction of a new calendar. Accordingly the Council issues the following declaration:

1. The Council is not opposed to the assignment of the feast of Easter to a particular Sunday of the Gregorian Calendar, provided those whom it may concern, especially other Christians who are not in communion with the Apostolic See, give their assent.

2. The Council likewise declares that it does not oppose measures designed to introduce a perpetual calendar into civil society.

Among the various systems being suggested to establish a perpetual calendar and to introduce it into civil life, only those systems are acceptable to the Church that retain and safeguard a seven-day week with Sunday and introduce no days outside the week, so that the present sequence of weeks is left intact, unless the most serious reasons arise. Concerning these the Apostolic See will make its own judgment.

The Fathers of the Council have given assent to all and to each part of the matters set forth in this Constitution. And together with the venerable Fathers, we, by the apostolic power given to us by Christ, approve, enact, and establish in the Holy Spirit each and all the decrees in this Constitution and command that what has been thus established in the Council be promulgated for the glory of God.

1. RomM, prayer over the gifts, Holy Thursday and 2d Sunday in Ordinary Time.

2. See Heb. 13:14.

3. See Eph. 2:21–22.

4. See Eph. 4:13.

5. See Is. 11:12.

6. See Jn. 11:52.

7. See Jn. 10:16.

Chapter I

1. See Is. 61:1; Lk. 4:18.

2. Ignatius of Antioch, *To the Ephesians* 7, 2.

3. See 1 Tm. 2:5.

4. *Sacramentarium Veronense* (ed. Mohlberg), n. 1265.

5. RomM, preface I of Easter.

6. RomM, prayer after the seventh reading, Easter Vigil.

7. See Mk. 16:15.

8. See Acts 26:18.

9. See Rom. 6:4, Eph. 2:6; Col. 3:1.

10. See Jn. 4:23.

11. See 1 Cor. 11:26.

12. Council of Trent, sess. 13, 11 Oct. 1551, *Decree on the Holy Eucharist*, chap. 5.

13. Council of Trent, sess. 22, 17 Sept. 1562, *Doctrine on the Holy Sacrifice of the Mass*, chap. 2.

14. See Augustine, *In Ioannis Evangelium Tractatus 6,* chap. 1, n. 7.

15. See Rv. 21:2; Col. 3:1; Heb. 8:2.

16. See Phil. 3:20; Col 3:4.

17. See Jn. 17:3; Lk. 24:47; Acts 2:38.

18. See Mt. 28:20.

19. RomM, prayer after communion, Easter Vigil.

20. RomM, opening prayer, mass for Monday of Easter Week.

21. See 2 Cor. 6:1.

22. See Mt. 6:6.

23. See 1 Thes. 5:17.

24. See 2 Cor. 4:10–11.

25. RomM, prayer over the gifts, Saturday after the 2d, 4th, and 6th Sundays of Easter.

26. Cyprian, *On the Unity of the Catholic Church 7;* see *Letter 66,* n. 8, 3.

27. See Council of Trent, sess. 22, 17 Sept. 1562, *Doctrine on the Holy Sacrifice of the Mass,* chap. 8.

28. See Ignatius of Antioch, *To the Magnesians,* 7; *To the Philadelphians,* 4; *To the Smyrnians,* 8.

Chapter II

1. See Augustine, *In Ioannis Evangelium Tractatus 36,* chap. 6, n. 13.

2. Liturgy of the Hours, antiphon for Canticle of Mary, evening prayer II, feast of Corpus Christi.

3. See Cyril of Alexandria, *Commentary on the Gospel of John,* book 11, chap. 11–12.

4. See 1 Tm. 2:1–2.

5. Council of Trent, sess. 21, *Doctrine on Communion under Both Species,* chap. 1–3.

Chapter III

1. Council of Trent, sess. 24, *Decree on Reform,* chap. 1. See also RomR, title 8, chap. 2, n. 6.

Chapter VI

1. See Eph. 5:19; Col. 3:16.

About the Liturgical Institute

The Liturgical Institute, founded in 2000 by His Eminence Francis Cardinal George of Chicago, offers a variety of options for education in Liturgical Studies. A unified, rites-based core curriculum constitutes the foundation of the program, providing integrated and balanced studies toward the advancement of the renewal promoted by the Second Vatican Council. The musical, artistic, and architectural dimensions of worship are given particular emphasis in the curriculum. Institute students are encouraged to participate in its "liturgical heart" of daily Mass and Morning and Evening Prayer. The academic program of the Institute serves a diverse, international student population—laity, religious, and clergy—who are preparing for service in parishes, dioceses, and religious communities. Personalized mentoring is provided in view of each student's ministerial and professional goals. The Institute is housed on the campus of the University of St. Mary of the Lake/Mundelein Seminary, which offers the largest priestly formation program in the United States and is the center of the permanent diaconate and lay ministry training programs of the Archdiocese of Chicago. In addition, the University has the distinction of being the first chartered institution of higher learning in Chicago (1844), and one of only seven pontifical faculties in North America.

For more information about the Liturgical Institute and its programs, contact: usml.edu/liturgicalinstitute. Phone: 847-837-4542. E-mail: litinst@usml.edu.

Msgr. Reynold Hillenbrand
1904-1979

Monsignor Reynold Hillenbrand, ordained a priest by Cardinal George Mundelein in 1929, was Rector of St. Mary of the Lake Seminary from 1936 to 1944.

He was a leading figure in the liturgical and social action movement in the United States during the 1930s and worked to promote active, intelligent, and informed participation in the Church's liturgy.

He believed that a reconstruction of society would occur as a result of the renewal of the Christian spirit, whose source and center is the liturgy.

Hillenbrand taught that, since the ultimate purpose of Catholic action is to Christianize society, the renewal of the liturgy must undoubtedly play the key role in achieving this goal.

Hillenbrand Books strives to reflect the spirit of Monsignor Reynold Hillenbrand's pioneering work by making available innovative and scholarly resources that advance the liturgical and sacramental life of the Church.